CARMICHAEL

FOR THE CHILDREN OF INDIA

SAM WELLMAN

BARBOUR
PUBLISHING

Amy
CARMICHAEL

ISBN 1-59310-380-8

All Scripture quotations are taken from the King James Version of the Bible.

Cover illustration © Dick Bobnick
Cover design by Douglas Miller (mhpubarts.com)

Published by Barbour Publishing, Inc., P.O. Box 719, Uhrichsville, Ohio 44683, www.barbourbooks.com

Our mission is to publish and distribute inspirational products offering exceptional value and biblical encouragement to the masses.

Member of the
Evangelical Christian
Publishers Association

Printed in the United States of America.
5 4 3 2

half a mile upstream on the same creek. The stream had been dammed just beyond the second mill, creating a pool of slack water. How well she knew that murky vastness. Her father had tied a rope around her waist and held the other end as Amy thrashed about in water that felt as unyielding as a slurry of concrete. But eventually she began to "swim." Or at least she could dog-paddle to safety in an emergency. Norman and Ernest passed the same ordeal. And so it was with every Carmichael child. Of course, the sea was quite a different challenge. Once, Amy and her brothers were rowing a small boat in the long tidal channel near Portaberry, where Grandmother Filson lived. The current caught the boat and swept it toward the open sea. Amy began to beseech God with a hymn:

> *He leadeth me, O blessed thought,*
> *O words with heavenly comfort fraught;*
> *Whate'er I do, where'er I be,*
> *Still 'tis God's hand that leadeth me!*[3]

Frightened, Norman and Ernest joined in at the top of their lungs as their small arms cranked the oars against the current. Just as the rowboat seemed destined to cross the bar into the open sea, a coast-guard lifeboat rescued them. God had surely answered Amy's plea. Life seemed lost, then found again, and Amy would never forget looking death in the face. But it was a good thing Norman and Ernest quickly forgot their brushes with death with their brash older sister, "or else they might not be so willing to follow me in my next adventure," she admitted.

In the middle of the reservoir at the mill where Amy

merely burbled in his crib.

To think the little wretch has blue eyes!

She had prayed for blue eyes. "Please come and sit with me,"[1] she had said to Jesus as she did every night, smoothing a place on the sheet beside her. Welcoming Jesus into her bed was her very first memory. One night when she was young, she had asked Jesus for blue eyes. Mother had said that Jesus hears our prayers and answers them. But no, in her mirror the next morning her eyes remained brown as dirt. Later, much later, she wrote:

> Where, O where
>   Could the blue eyes be? Not there;
> Jesus hadn't answered.
>   Hadn't answered her at all;
> Never more
>   Could she pray; her eyes were brown
> As before.
>   Did a little soft wind blow?
> Came a whisper soft and low,
>   Jesus answered. He said, "No". . .[2]

Like a bright ray of the sun on a gloomy day she had realized His answer was "No." That didn't make it any less disappointing. Her mother had eyes as blue as forget-me-nots. So did her brother. Maybe that disappointment explained her peculiar torment of him. For she would pinch him until the tears glistened in his angry eyes.

"Lord, forgive me," said Amy, remembering, "but the pain caused the most gorgeous sapphire blue!"

She glanced over at the great mill that sat near a creek that emptied into the sea. There was a second mill the pony rested, Amy examined the tidal pools. The shoreline seemed to be God's creation in the raw: "plants," which her father said were really animals, clung to the rocks and swayed in the surging surf; stalk-eyed crabs skittered in the shallow pools left by the retreating tide; mute, blind, deaf clams sent their bubbling breath to the surface of the sand. All these creatures thrived in a sea that appeared chaotic from the distance but on close inspection was clear and teeming with life. As the ocean ebbed and flowed, the creatures moved endlessly to and fro, only to eventually pass out of existence. Could such exquisite creatures be accidents?

"That's too silly!" snapped Amy.

She brushed aside the heavy thoughts and watched with rapt attention as a snail oozed across an open space between the rocks. Its helical shell seemed a royal design. Yes, how Amy loved animals. At home she had cleared her dollhouse of the insipid, rosy-cheeked, glassy-eyed dolls, replacing them with beetles and crickets. She had substituted moss and rocks for the tiny chairs and beds that furnished no comfort to her insects. A mouse or a toad would have been a nice addition, but Amy knew that her nursemaid, Bessie, would complain to Mother.

Amy studied the endless sea. She loved the color blue. The sea was so peaceful when it was blue. She remembered watching the sea from her nursery window on the second floor of the old house, when she must have been three years old. A green sea was an angry sea. A gray sea was an anxious sea. But a blue sea was peaceful. The sky was peaceful, too, when it was blue. She had told Norman her great discovery about colors, but he had

ONE

S teady there, girl," murmured twelve-year-old Amy
Beatrice Carmichael one summer day in 1880 along
the Irish Sea.

She patted her pony's sweaty neck. Its barreled sides
were heaving. Although most of the shore was rocky,
Amy knew the soft spots well. She had ridden the small
animal hard through the sandy patches. She surveyed the
rubble-strewn shore to make sure Norman and Ernest
weren't lurking about. They could be ornery to be sure,
especially when trying to even the score with Amy for
some delicious trick she had pulled on them. They knew
Fanny was a frisky pony who had thrown Amy more than
once when startled. Confident that her two younger
brothers were not nearby, Amy dismounted.

"Nice filly," she said soothingly.

Amy loved animals, and as she grew older, Amy found
herself returning more often to the beach to ride. While

learned to swim was a tiny one-tree island. This rather insignificant feature gave her home village its name: Millisle. The mills were very old, first bought by James Carmichael, Amy's ancestor, in 1705. James was from Ayr, in southwest Scotland. He was a staunch Presbyterian, too, one of those Scots who defied the English kings who wanted to shove the Church of England down their throats. It was no surprise that the Carmichaels had crossed the Irish Sea to practice their faith in northern Ireland.

The mills were now run by her father, David, and his brother William. They had modernized the mill machinery with steel rollers for milling the hard wheat imported from America, but some of the Irish were now importing American wheat already ground into flour, a development that worried her father and her uncle very much. But none of this seemed relevant to twelve-year-old Amy as she sat and dreamed near a tidal pool.

"First memories are so scrumptious," she mused, trying to get her reflections back on track.

Once again, the first memories came into her mind from the nursery—and the sea. Sounds. First sounds. The wind cooing down the flue of the nursery chimney. The surge of waves even on the calmest day. Wasting this calm, warm day suddenly jolted her.

"Come on, Fanny; let's ride," she said as she remounted the rested beast.

She rode Fanny into a lather again and then trotted the pony back to her home. Most houses in Millisle were tiny-windowed stone cottages. But the two Carmichael clans, David's and William's, lived in two of the three largest houses in Millisle. David's was a two-story house of gray stone, with fireplaces on each end. Bay windows and dormers spoke of money and privilege, almost as much as the walled grounds with apple trees and rose-bushes. Amy and her brothers and sisters were taught by a governess. Other than her five cousins—all deemed un-ruly roughnecks by her mother—she saw other children in the village only when she went to their cottages on a mission of mercy with a pot of soup or when she saw them in the Presbyterian church. The village children must have liked her, because often before church they of-fered her peppermint candy.

"Thank you very much, but my mother would rather I didn't," she had to primly refuse.[4]

The refusal haunted her during the two-hour service as the sweet, faint smell wafted to her pew. The other children not only sucked on candy, but they were also al-lowed to lie down in the pews. Not Amy, or Norman, Ernest, Eva, Ethel, Walter, or Alfred. The Carmichaels sat upright. It wasn't possible to stretch out, not even if one resolved to suffer the consequences later. Punishment for slouching in church was swift as lightning.

Amy's thoughts came back to the present as she led Fanny into the stable. "There, filly, have some hay."

She curried the animal as her father had taught her. Being indifferent to the needs of an animal was a sin. "A righteous man regardeth the life of his beast: but the tender mercies of the wicked are cruel," says Proverbs 12:10. Amy was sure the verse applied to any animal. She had rescued a squeaking mouse once from the rain barrel. Oh, how perfectly Bobby Burns had posed it:

Wee, sleekit, cow'rin, tim'rous beastie,
O what a panic's in thy breastie!

10

Another time, Amy had thrown a fit when a cousin tortured a frog. That was a memory she could live without. The wicked boy had impaled the frog on some thorns, and the thought of terrible thorns like that tearing the flesh of Jesus sickened her. But, praise God, most of her animal memories were tender ones. Daisy the cat and Gildo the collie had the run of the Carmichael estate. They were family pets, like Fanny and the other pony, Charlie. Amy now noticed that Charlie was gone, which probably meant that pesky Norman and Ernest were being bounced around somewhere in the village. Good. Perhaps she could enjoy some quiet reading at her desk.

"If Ethel and Eva and Walter and Alfred don't bother me," she grumbled.

Back in her bedroom, which she shared with her two young sisters, Eva and Ethel, she sat at the desk. Long ago, Norman and Ernest had slept in this same room with Amy—the "nursery," Mother called it then—but now the two older brothers slept with the two younger brothers, Walter and Alfred, in the boys' bedroom. There were seven Carmichael children in all, and a deep weariness in Mother's eyes hinted to Amy there would not be an eighth.

Mother was loving but stern, too. Not that Amy herself was some sort of saint, she reflected, but it seemed she had taken more than her share of punishment. "Pink tea" was an ever-looming threat—if Mother had the time. A lesser punishment was a ruler across the palm, after which Amy was required to politely thank her mother. Another form of correction was standing in a corner with nothing to see but the dreary wall. And, of course, an instant, skin-burning spanking was only an arm's length away, if Mother was pressed for time or really angry. Once, Amy had climbed up through a skylight to march around on the slate roof for a while. If Norman and Ernest hadn't tagged behind her and yipped and yiped enough to rouse the entire village, she wouldn't have been caught and summarily spanked.

"If only they knew what a rogue I *could* be," muttered Amy many a time, when neither parent could hear her.

When Amy looked in the mirror, she saw thick brown hair framing an oval, milky-skinned face with a turned-up nose and brown eyes. This was the demure Amy that her mother wanted other people to see. But did astute observers notice that Amy's eyes were not the placid liquid browns of a deer but the sparkling, mischievous eyes of a fox? With little effort, in private, she could beetle her brows into a face any demon would be pleased to wear or into a mask of trust. This latter look was surely the face that enchanted Norman and Ernest onto the roof of the house that day. It was surely the face that urged Norman and Ernest to row into the tidal channel at Portaberry. It was surely the face that induced her two brothers to stand on the sea wall with her one windy day as the salty spray drenched their clothing. And it was surely the face that encouraged her two brothers to eat suspicious-looking seeds from the garden.

"Well, they survived, *this time!*" barked her mother. "But it's 'pink tea' time for you, young lady!"

She would watch as Mother mixed a nasty pink powder into a little cup of hot water. It gave quite a stomachache to be sure, but complaining to Mother about the pain did no good at all. The potion was intended to give pain.

"I hope it will do you good,"[5] murmured her mother.

TWO

Although her parents—especially her mother—punished without fail and did not express love in a tender way, the house was full of love. Mr. Carmichael often took his children away from the house and grounds to wander the village of Millisle and its surroundings. He introduced Amy to her first clovered field and her first tidal pool. The children never lacked for pets and toys and books. Yes, books they had in plenty. When Amy was very young, her parents had read to her. When it wasn't the Bible or the Shorter Catechism, it was usually tales of Christian martyrs. Of course, martyrs of Scotland were emphasized, from Patrick Hamilton in 1527 to Walter Mill in 1558. The legends of Robin Hood and King Arthur seemed to have been served to Amy with her mother's milk, as were Mother Goose stories and Aesop's fables. Shakespeare was spoon-fed in the form of Charles Lamb's *Tales of Shakespeare*.

When the children were old enough to read on their

own, the richness in the Carmichael library seemed inexhaustible. Among Amy's favorites was *The Pilgrim's Progress*; and the story of its author, John Bunyan, a simple tinker, was almost as uplifting as the Christian allegory of salvation itself. *Robinson Crusoe* was not as essential but contained the stuff of dreams. What to do on a deserted island? *Gulliver's Travels* was available, too; and no child of Amy's day could miss *Alice's Adventures in Wonderland* and *Through the Looking Glass*. And like any good girl of Scottish descent, Amy enjoyed George Macdonald's *At the Back of the North Wind*:

> Diamond walked towards her instantly. When he reached her knees, he put out his hand to lay it on her, but nothing was there save an intense cold. He walked on. Then all grew white about him; and the cold stung him like fire. He walked on still, groping through the whiteness. It thickened about him. . .he felt swallowed up in whiteness. It was when he reached North Wind's heart that he fainted and fell. But as he fell, he rolled over the threshold, and it was thus that Diamond got to the back of the north wind. . . .

Amy knew early on that Macdonald's writing was not the best, yet his storytelling overwhelmed any literary inadequacies. Novels by Sir Walter Scott never raised a parent's eyebrow, but borrowed literature such as the Victorian novels of Jane Eyre and Charlotte Brontë or the American imports *Little Women* and *Tom Sawyer* would draw a suspicious frown from Mother. Any Irish writer, except a Protestant like Maria Edgeworth, would draw an immediate rebuke from Amy's parents.

Poetry thrilled her most of all. It soared high above prose in its brilliance. The majestic poetry of John Milton was certainly encouraged. Poetry by Bobby Burns or George Herbert was not suspect. But John Donne and William Blake were close to crossing the line. In Blake's "Auguries of Innocence," Amy was entranced by certain verses; to wit:

> To see a World in a grain of sand,
> And a Heaven in a wild flower,
> Hold infinity in the palm of your hand,
> And eternity in an hour.

When occasionally Amy was able to read Irish poets, she was often startled by their fiery hatred of England. She read the works of many suspect poets, as well as all the expected. In addition to the great changes from Milton to Wordsworth and from Wordsworth to Tennyson, she began to discern subtle differences between contemporaries like Robert Browning and Matthew Arnold. Smitten, she wrote poetry herself. Her rhyme and meter clunked woodenly, but she persisted. And the more poetry she read, the better her own poetry became. Oh, to create poetry like George Herbert or even like the wild, wild William Blake!

Oh, to read poetry and ride horseback along the rocky shores! What a very happy childhood Amy had! And yet, she had worried for some time that the end of her childish reverie might soon be approaching. When the inevitable news was finally announced at supper one night, the realization was a thousand times harder to bear.

"Must I?" she asked her mother, as a lump as big as a watermelon seemed to form in Amy's throat.

"I'm afraid you must," her mother answered coolly. "Let's

Amy CARMICHAEL

not make a fuss."

So one day late in the summer of 1880, her luggage packed with clothing, Amy said good-bye to her mother and her six brothers and sisters and stepped into a carriage to begin her journey to boarding school. Her father accompanied her to the docks in Belfast, fifteen miles due west. As a poetic device, the direction west was death, and Amy felt its figurative truth. She kissed her father good-bye and was off on a steamship, east as it turned out, across the Irish Sea to England. Well-to-do "British" families deemed such remote schooling necessary.

Upon first seeing her destination, Amy muttered with dread, "Marlborough House."

The girls' boarding school in the large town of Harrogate was run by Methodists. Crossing denominational lines obviously didn't bother Amy's parents. They were from a Presbyterian background, but they were not such staunch Calvinists that they had a problem with John Wesley's Methodism. If one could set aside the question of predestination, both were holy equals. Nor did her parents have a problem with Quakers or any other devout group. Their concerns were to believe God's Word in the Bible and to accept His Son as their Savior.

"We hard-nosed Ulster Irish do not puzzle over questions like 'How many angels can dance on the head of a pin?'" Amy told her startled classmates.

Harrogate was in the uplands. Mineral springs had been discovered in the area more than three hundred years before, and many came there to enjoy their recuperative powers. Below Harrogate, the rise between the Nidd and the Wharfe rivers slipped down to the larger town of York. This ancient city, called Eboracum by the Romans, still had its medieval

17

walls and four great gates. Each gate comprised a series of
barriers that had to be raised. Below the arched stone gateway, trapdoors once lay over deep, cruel pits. Hidden within
the gateway were "murder holes," where boiling oil and a
dozen other excruciatingly painful ways of killing men were
unleashed. The most decisive battle of the English civil war
had been fought in nearby Marston Moor, where on July 2,
1644, Oliver Cromwell had thrashed the first King Charles.
York also boasted York Minster, an old Gothic cathedral
with more medieval glass than any other church in England.

"It seems hate and violence and heroism and worship
were all heightened in these ancients," Amy shuddered.

She learned much English history from her surroundings. She had been sheltered from much of it in Millisle.
Even as Amy went to school, a new chapter in Irish history
was being unveiled. She learned that reforms passed in the
English Parliament had not satisfied the Irish. They wanted
self-rule. Their champion, Charles Parnell, urged the Irish
not to pay land rents to the British. For that rebellious act,
he was arrested and imprisoned. Then he struck a deal with
William Gladstone, the current prime minister of Great
Britain, only to have it disintegrate when Irish revolutionar-
ies murdered British officials in Dublin, Ireland.

Among her English schoolmates, Amy preferred to
change the subject from politics to something more to her
liking. "Botany is the only subject I like," she told her peers.

Her interest in botany apparently blossomed in her
dormitory window, where she nurtured lilies and chrysanthemums from her native soil. Of course, as the oldest
child, she had been nurturing her whole life in the role of
"little mother" to her brothers and sisters, and her habits
prevailed in her new environment as well. At school she not

only socialized among her peers but regimented them. She led by example. If the girls desired a certain dessert, it was Amy who brashly approached the cook and persuaded her to prepare it. In admiration, the other girls said she was "wild Irish," which amused Amy.

Another incident that characterized her role as "ring-leader" in the dormitory occurred one night when the girls wanted to stay up late to watch a particularly brilliant comet. When Amy and her dormitory mates were told by Miss Kay, the principal, that curfew would not be relaxed, Amy devised a plan to awaken her friends in time to see the comet. She tied strings to the toes of all her dormitory mates, then stayed awake until it was time to rouse the others by pulling on the strings. Amy and all the other girls were caught by Miss Kay, who staked out the attic where the girls gathered; but she relented and allowed them to see the comet!

Back in the dormitory, Amy said breezily, "Well, girls, now you can tell your grandchildren you saw the great comet of 1882!"

But once lights were out for the night and Amy was lying alone in her dormitory bed, her exhilaration at seeing celestial grandeur turned to gloom. Certainly, as instigator of the disobedience, she would be summoned by the principal the next morning and expelled, bringing shame on her parents. Her misery brought remorse. Oh, why hadn't she studied harder? Now surely she would lose her one opportunity forever. *Oh, God in heaven, spare me this disgrace,* she prayed. And miraculously the next day brought her no reprimand at all. Yet she quickly forgot the incident and God's mercy and continued to idle through her schoolwork. At times, she seemed little more than a prisoner at Marlborough House.

In the spring of 1884, she sang in the choir at the

meetings of the Children's Special Service Mission. Mr. Edwin Arrowsmith had them sing a simple hymn—an import from America—that had become popular:

> *Jesus loves me! This I know,*
>   *for the Bible tells me so.*
> *Little ones to Him belong;*
>   *they are weak but He is strong.*

The first verse sang to Amy's heart like a thousand angels! Did she know she belonged to Jesus? The chorus spoke to her just as grandly:

> *Yes, Jesus loves me! Yes, Jesus loves me!*
>   *Yes, Jesus loves me! The Bible tells me so.*

Jesus loved her. Of course the Bible had told her that. But had she accepted that love? She knew by now how the Wesleys had stressed a second sanctification in a Christian's development. But it seemed mumbo jumbo to Amy. The last verse of the hymn resonated in her heart:

> *Jesus loves me! He will stay*
>   *close beside me all the way.*
> *Thou has bled and died for me;*
>   *I will henceforth live for Thee.*[1]

After the hymn, Mr. Arrowsmith asked the children to be silent for several minutes. Amy brooded. What if what the Wesleys had said was true? Was this her second chance? Did she have to "accept" Jesus? As far as she could remember, she had not once actually asked Jesus to come into her heart. The

Amy CARMICHAEL

pain He bore on the cross seemed to crush her. Yes, she would open her heart to Jesus. Then it happened. Suddenly her chains fell away! She was soaring. The years in England that had seemed to her so empty, such a void, took on special meaning now. She had come into the desert as a pilgrim; and away from the distractions of human love at home, she had found God.

"I opened my heart to Him and in His great mercy the Good Shepherd has drawn me into His fold!"

At the end of that school year in 1884, her father came to the boarding school to take Amy to visit London before they both returned to Ireland. London was the greatest city in the world at that time, in every way. More than three million people inhabited the city, compared to one million in New York City at that time. London had a glorious history many times longer than any American borough, preserved in blood and paper and stone. Amy saw as much as could be seen in a few days, including Westminster Abbey, the British Museum, the Tower of London, St. Paul's Cathedral, Buckingham Palace, and Windsor Castle. She never caught a glimpse of Queen Victoria; but in the houses of Parliament, Father pointed out the white locks and craggy face of Prime Minister William Gladstone.

Amy's father soon revealed the purpose of the trip to London. It was possibly Amy's last chance to see such things. Her school days in England were at an end. The mills in Millisle had become unprofitable. There was no future in grinding American wheat, because the market was flooded with imported American flour. Her father and Uncle William were building a new mill near Belfast; and because the family also had to move to College Gardens to be near the new mill, money would be tight for a while. Norman and

Ernest were being withdrawn from their boarding schools as well. Amy now appreciated her schooling as never before.

"I loved all my teachers," she said. "Why didn't I study harder when I had the chance? I let everyone down as well as myself."

Amy was ashamed of her performance as a boarding student. She had indulged her "wildness" and wasted her chance at a higher education, a chance her four younger brothers and sisters might never get. She would just as soon forget her shortcomings; but back in Ireland, Amy did not forget her decision to accept Jesus as her Savior. But how was she to serve Him? A girl of sixteen had few options. At home she was once again the "little mother" to Ethel, Alfred, and Walter. Amy went calling socially with Mother, too. She participated in homespun charities, carrying food to the destitute and the elderly.

One experience made her heart ache. Her mother indulged her with a visit to a Belfast tea shop. While sitting at a table sipping tea and sampling sweet delicacies she didn't want, Amy noticed a face pressed against the window. *How charming,* she thought, *to see a little girl peering in at the sweets.* But when they left the tea shop, Amy saw that it was raining, and the girl's dress was very thin and dirty. With shock Amy realized that the ragamuffin girl was barefoot! Barefoot on a cold, drizzly day. So cold, so hungry, so poor, so sad!

"Oh, how could I have thought there was any charm in being so desperately poor?" she lamented.

In the cozy warmth of her bedroom that night, she set her feelings to verse.

> *When I grow up and money have,*
> *I know what I will do,*

I'll build a great big lovely place
  For little girls like you.[2]

"And yet at present I do nothing 'for little girls like you,'" she admitted. "Please, God, tell me what to do."

Weeks later, she was in Belfast on yet another gray, drizzly day, this time on a Sunday morning. After the service at the Rosemary Street Presbyterian Church, she saw an old lady on the street who was struggling to carry a heavy bundle. "Let's help her," Amy impulsively urged Norman and Ernest. So the three helped, one brother carrying the bundle and the other two escorting the old lady along. But when they ran into more and more people on the street who were leaving church services, Amy became embarrassed. Eyebrows were raised. The old lady was dirty and shabbily dressed. *Surely,* Amy thought, *these well-dressed people don't think we Carmichaels are somehow associated with this wretched old woman.* Oh, why had she been so impulsive? Amy became more and more exasperated, blushing as red as an apple, she was sure, by the time they passed a square with a great fountain.

Then words struck her ears like a thunderclap!

A voice boomed, "'Now if any man build upon this foundation gold, silver, precious stones, wood, hay, stubble; every man's work shall be made manifest: for the day shall declare it, because it shall be revealed by fire; and the fire shall try every man's work of what sort it is. If any man's work abide which he hath built thereupon, he shall receive a reward.'"

First Corinthians 3:12–14, thought Amy numbly.

But who had said it?

THREE

A my glanced around. All she saw were people bust-ling along the street. Now she was frightened. Was this some kind of mystical experience? Surely such things didn't happen to everyday people like herself. Not voices! Norman and Ernest showed no sign of having heard anything. She had to bite her tongue not to tell them. They would think she was crazy. That afternoon, back in College Gardens, she retired to her room. All the rest of the day she asked herself over and over whether God had spoken to her. Was such a thing possible? Wouldn't a rational person think it was merely Amy scolding herself in her anxiety? But after many hours, she acknowledged that she had heard the voice. She was certain. The incident could mean only one thing: " 'the fire shall try every man's work of what sort it is.' The meaning of that is plain enough," she admitted.

And what had her work been? Gold or stubble? One charitable act had been required of her this day, and she had been mortified with embarrassment! *Stubble!* In His mercy God had warned her. *Oh God, let me serve You with gold,* she prayed. She would tell no one of the experience, but she would immediately begin to offer her gold—if she could presume to call the work she planned such an exalted thing.

First, Amy began to invite children of the neighborhood on Sunday afternoons to her home. There she regaled them with stories. They played games. Bible lessons were woven in the midst of the fun. She was not surprised when the children responded enthusiastically to her efforts. She had much experience entertaining younger children. Ethel, Alfred, and Walter attended, too, just as eagerly awaiting the fun as the others. But in her heart Amy knew these neighborhood children were privileged. They certainly deserved to know Jesus, but somehow it seemed that other children needed Jesus more. How could she doubt it? Hadn't she seen that innocent urchin peering through the tea-shop window?

"Peering at sweets the poor little thing could not have. . . ." Amy remembered a verse from George Herbert: " '*You must sit down,*' *says Love,* '*and taste my meat.*' " Oh, why hadn't she insisted to her mother that they invite the little girl into the tea shop for a sweet? And why did Amy not now invite the poor in to taste the Lord's meat?

Amy went to the Belfast City Mission and volunteered to go into the slums with the Reverend Henry Montgomery on Saturday nights. *Oh God, give me the strength and courage to make a difference,* she prayed. Amy began to approach children who were loitering on the street. "Come with us and let us sing and tell stories," she said to them with a warm smile.

"What for?" they asked suspiciously.

"Fun," she replied with a laugh. A handful of them did come! Of course, the meat of God's Word was always sandwiched in the middle of fun things to do. Oh, indescribable joy! But not indescribable power. Her power came from Jesus. She knew that. The handful grew to dozens as the word spread. Why wander around with nothing do? There was a young woman over at the City Mission who knew how to have fun! Amy did not even mind being teased a bit. Teasing was just an impish form of friendship. Any difficult children she bore with a loving smile.

But she quickly corrected sins. "Don't you know the words, child, of Saint Peter? 'For he that will love life, and see good days, let him refrain his tongue from evil, and his lips that they speak no guile.' So don't you go around telling stories on people." Even then Amy was smiling.

Her efforts grew, always injecting the Word of God into the fun. Soon she was teaching a group of boys at night. She knew children did not love to be "organized," but they did love to belong to an organization. She started another program she called "Morning Watch," in which the slum children pledged to regularly read the Bible and pray. To seal the bargain, each child signed their very own gilt-edged blue pledge card. Every Saturday morning the Morning Watch children met to discuss their week's successes or failures. And, of course, they had fun, too, so much fun that Alfred and Walter were soon Morning Watchers as well.

Her prayer group for girls soon became so large it had to be moved to Victoria College. Every night, Amy thanked God that He gave her such power with children. And Amy's power also attracted older children, even some young women. These were the mill girls, the girls too poor to wear the fancy hats of the day. They covered their heads in public with their shawls and thus were called "shawlies." Amy drew these girls and young women from the slums to the Presbyterian church on Rosemary Street. Almost hidden in her efforts to teach them hygiene and etiquette, she taught them to read the Bible and pray.

"Ernest," she said one day to her brother, who now worked on the railroad, "what do you know of the shawlies?"

Ernest hesitated. "But we are told never to gossip."

"Then tell me what you truly know, for 'the truth shall make you free.' "

So Ernest told her what he truly knew. That was horrifying enough. Unmarried shawlies with babies were common. Ernest had seen them with his own eyes. And common, too, was the crime of men molesting the shawlies. Often it came down to just how hard the girl could kick and scratch and scream. That Ernest had seen with his own eyes, too. And the gossip he couldn't repeat was a thousand times worse. Many of the shawlies were mired in a living nightmare.

Amy's heart ached. "We Carmichaels have so much, and they have so little."

Amy knew she must try harder than ever to give these girls hope, but her own world was shaken again. Her father had looked ill for several months. In the spring of 1885, Amy, who was by now seventeen, saw him talking to Mother in the dining room. The subject was money, and Father had never looked so sick. He had loaned a very large amount of the family money to someone. It seemed now the family would never get it back. That bad judgment seemed to be crushing Amy's father. Soon he was bedridden. On April 8, a Wednesday, the traditional day for singing hymns—he asked his family to sing "My Faith Looks Up to Thee." The last verse ran:

> When ends life's transient dream,
>   when death's cold sullen stream
>   shall o'er me roll,
> Blest Savior, then, in love,
>   fear and distrust remove—
> O bear me safe above,
>   a ransomed soul.[1]

Was it possible that Amy's father sensed the end? He was only fifty-four years old. She had just traveled the year before with him in England. He seemed all right then. Yet on Sunday morning, April 12, David Carmichael died as the church bells were ringing. It was as if he willed it.

"Surely Father built some gold on the foundation," sobbed Amy in her room after the funeral.

She continued her labors, now dressed in the somber winter colors of mourning. The household rose at 4:50 a.m. these days. For breakfast they ate brown and white bread, fresh sliced or toasted, with marmalade. Often they had bacon, too; and on Sundays they had smoked fish called *finnan haddie.* Supper was usually bread, potatoes, and sausage or fish. With every meal they drank tea. Their table had suffered a little since Father's death. No longer were Grandmother's occasional offerings from Portaberry of turkey and such treats taken with an air of nonchalance. Now their arrival was an event of great interest.

But the Carmichaels were scarcely destitute. Many of the truly poor in Ireland virtually lived on potatoes. That was the reason the blight of the 1840s that caused the harvested potatoes to rot in their cellars was so catastrophic. The poor starved by the hundreds of thousands. No, the Carmichaels had never suffered like that.

In September 1886, Amy took a ship across the Irish Sea to Scotland to visit an old school friend.

"Come with me to Glasgow," her friend urged her, "where the faithful are convening meetings there—along 'Keswick lines.'"

"Keswick lines?"

Amy learned what "Keswick" meant. In 1875, in Cumberland, one of England's most northern counties, a convention was held in a large tent at Broadlands, the estate of W. Cowper-Temple, in the village of Keswick in England's tranquil lake district. One of the sponsors was Robert Wilson, a man wealthy from his coal mines in Cumberland. Also in attendance in that first meeting had been the writer George Macdonald. The purpose of the convention was a return to holiness and an opportunity for spiritual healing. All discussions of forming a new sect were forbidden. Discussions of doctrine were discouraged, yet an informal "Keswick" doctrine had developed over the ten years since then. Keswick participants generally rejected a common notion that, although the believer is justified in an instant, he must struggle for years for sanctification. Keswick people believed sanctification could come in an instant, too, in a "second blessing."

Amy went with her friend to the meeting in Glasgow, certainly hoping and praying for such a moment. Neither speaker the day she was there affected her at all. But in the closing prayer, the minister paraphrased part of verse 24 of the book of Jude. "Lord, we know Thou are able to keep us from falling."

Yes, "unto him that is able to keep you from falling," she reflected. The rest of the verse in Jude popped into Amy's mind. Yes, the Lord was able to present us in His glory without fault and with exceeding joy, too. Oh yes, glory and majesty, dominion and power, now and forever. Amy left the meeting slightly dazed. It was odd how some things moved her and some did not. It reminded her of the sermon she heard at Harrogate—completely forgotten now—that had been followed by singing the hymn "Jesus Loves Me." That hymn thrilled her every time she thought of it. And sitting in a restaurant with her friend after the Glasgow meeting, the verse she heard struck her again: "Unto him that is able to keep you from falling." Now it seemed momentous. Was this the instant? Was this her second blessing?

In the flyleaf of her Bible, she wrote at the top left the words, "Thou Shalt Remember." Below that line she wrote "Glasgow Sept. 23, 1886." Below that she wrote the part of verse 24 from Jude that now thrilled her so: "Unto him that is able to keep you from falling."

But was she transformed in any way? And how did one know? Long ago Charles Wesley had known his "second blessing," because the next morning he had awakened so full of joy and love he was singing a hymn! But Amy had no such dramatic scene. When Amy returned to Belfast, the season of mourning for her father was over. Her mother took Amy to dress shops to update her wardrobe, but Amy spurned the new clothes. Such finery was vanity. All the frills and sashes and ribbons filled her with revulsion. Her thoughts echoed Saint Paul's first letter to Timothy: "In like manner also, that women adorn themselves in modest apparel, with shamefacedness and sobriety; not with broided hair, or gold, or pearls, or costly array; but (which becometh women professing godliness) with good works." Amy realized with a start that some very fundamental change had happened to her in Glasgow. She was bent on living and breathing God's Word, bent on leading a new life of discipleship.

Her disdain for "the world and its applause" did not sour her enjoyment of her family. As a recreation, she proposed a family news "magazine" called *Scraps*. All seven siblings had to contribute under pen names. Norman was "Namron," Ernest was "Oddfellow," Eva chose "Lulu," Ethel wrote as "Atom," Walter was "Blanco," and Alfred coined the acronym "SSI," for Silly Silly Idiot. Amy had read somewhere that the "i-a-n" at the end of "Christian" should stand for "I am nobody," so in *Scraps*, Amy became "Nobody."

The eight siblings contributed anecdotes, cartoons, drawings, poetry, and anything else they thought worthy of an evening's discussion. Amy—that is, "Nobody"—especially liked to contribute sketches and poetry. Her sketches were usually botanical: ferns, flowers, and grasses. One sketch revealed an ambition. She designed the dust jacket for a book titled *Mill Girls and All About Them*. Needless to say, she was the author on the cover. One example of her poetry in *Scraps* was:

> *Think truly, and thy thoughts shall be*
> > *Spotless with God's own purity.*
> *On every thought-bud let us bear*
> > *The stamp of truth, and love and prayer.*[2]

"Nobody" was so bold as to publish character sketches of the Carmichaels in the Christmas issue of 1887. In describing the virtues of her brothers and sisters, Amy interjected that her own faults were so numerous and so outweighed other people's faults that the less said of herself, the better! She concluded her study by lauding her mother as "perfect in every way" but pointed out that Mother was a woman shadowed in grief whose life they all had to brighten with their love.

In 1887 many of the "Keswick people" held meetings in Belfast and invited none other than Hudson Taylor. Taylor was the most famous missionary in the world, at least since the great David Livingstone had perished in Africa in 1873. Taylor had gone into China in the 1860s. His mission society was called the China Inland Mission. Most now just referred to it as the CIM. The CIM penetrated deeply into China; its missionaries wore native clothing and spoke native dialects. The society received enormous publicity in 1885 when the "Cambridge Seven," a group of noted athletes from Cambridge University, volunteered to serve in China.

Long ago the "father of Protestant Christian missions," England's own William Carey, had astounded the English with the enormity of the unsaved heathen population in the world: 557 million souls! "If God wants to convert the heathen, young man," cried a detractor, "He will do it without asking advice from you—or me!" But the detractor's resistance was trampled by the thousands of missionaries who went forth to India, China, and Africa. Still, the number of unsaved souls in the world grew even larger. Now it was Hudson Taylor who cried from the rooftops: the total was a staggering 865 million. Even more heartbreaking was the fact that, every day, fifty thousand of these souls died unsaved. Fifty thousand every day!

In *Scraps,* Amy wrote, "Does it not stir up our hearts to go forth and help them, does it not make us long to leave

our luxury, our exceeding abundant light, and go to them
that sit in darkness?"[3]

Amy was there at the 1887 meetings in Belfast with her
mother and aunts to hear it all. Her aunts were outspoken
and invited Robert Wilson, the coal tycoon and one of the
first organizers of the Keswick meetings, to come to their
house for a visit. Wilson obliged and seemed intensely moved
by the joy in the Carmichael home. He read his hosts a poem
by Frances Havergal, a very gifted hymnist who had recently
died at the young age of forty-three. She was called the "consecration poet," because of her dedication to living in Christ.
Wilson was a huge, bearded man, making his gentleness and
taciturn speech all the more noticeable. A Quaker, he simply
retreated into silence if pressed into an unpleasant exchange.
Amy respected his silence. His blue eyes and pinkish face
seemed as innocent as a child's. The humility in one of his
anecdotes especially impressed her.

"If stone in the quarry is hammered again and again,
which blow splits it? 'All of them,' you would say. And in
the same way you must never say, 'I won that soul for
Christ,' because it was won by the first witness for Christ
and the last witness for Christ and all those in between!"

Early in 1888, Mother announced during one of their
evening get-togethers that their funds were almost gone.
Amy felt no sorrow at all. God's Word prevented any self-
pity. Jesus Himself said it in the book of Matthew:

*Therefore take no thought, saying, What shall we
eat? or, What shall we drink? or, Wherewithal shall
we be clothed? (For after all these things do the Gen-
tiles seek:) for your heavenly Father knoweth that ye
have need of all these things. But seek ye first the*

kingdom of God, and his righteousness; and all these things shall be added unto you.

"Seek ye first the kingdom of God." What could be more clear than that? Amy learned that Robert Wilson had lost his only daughter, Rachel, a young lady about Amy's age. Perhaps that was why he looked at Amy in such a fatherly way. She was certainly struck by the fact that Robert Wilson was very nearly the age of her own departed father! When he had left the Carmichael home, Amy felt very strongly in her heart that she would see Robert Wilson again. Months later, she received a letter from him.

"Robert Wilson has invited me to the 1888 Keswick meeting!" she cried.

"You must go," said her mother.

In Keswick, Amy confirmed all she had heard. All doctrinal distractions were to be avoided. The object of Keswick was sanctity. The self must be subdued. Conquer the smallest sin. Put away all bitterness and rancor. Abide every hour in Christ. Call on divine power to strengthen every weakness. Robert Wilson and his friends could scarcely rub elbows with a firebrand like Hudson Taylor and not feel an obligation to save the heathen. When the Keswick Society decided to start the funding necessary to send forth missionaries sometime in the future, Amy found herself strangely excited.

Do I dare think of myself as a candidate for such an honor? she wondered.

Yet Amy became more agitated, too. Didn't the call to evangelize the unsaved heathen interfere with what she was doing in Belfast? It seemed so. In the flyleaf of her Bible this time she wrote from Paul's second letter to the Corinthians,

"And he said unto me, 'My grace is sufficient for thee: for my strength is made perfect in weakness.' Most gladly therefore will I rather glory in my infirmities, that the power of Christ may rest upon me." When she wrote the words, she repeated "of Christ," revealing her confusion and troubled thoughts. And she added part of a verse from Psalm 121: "from this time forth, and even for evermore." She had omitted the first half of the verse: "The Lord shall preserve thy going out and thy coming in." *Why?* she wondered later. Could she not put to paper the thought of "going out"? Was such a thing too much of a commitment? Did she love her work in Belfast too much?

If the Lord calls me to go forth, am I unwilling? she asked herself.

Back in Belfast, Amy soon was having a problem with her shawlies that she would never have imagined at the beginning of her efforts.

FOUR

Shawlies came to Amy's meetings in such great numbers that they could no longer be accommodated by the church that let her use its facilities. In the church magazine, *The Christian*, Amy read of a large hall, prefabricated from sheet metal, that could be erected for five hundred English pounds.

"Do I dare dream of building our own hall?" she asked.

She urged her girls to pray "unto him that is able to keep you from falling." But she also recalled an experience from her past. She had been staying with Grandmother Filson in Portaberry. Amy, virtually a native of that village, went out to collect for the poor. She knew of one man who would surely give her some money. He had just built himself a fine house. But no! With a scowl, he shooed her away. He couldn't love God. The implications were enormous.

"People who do not love God are just a distraction to my mission," she told herself then. "I must pray to God to move

36

people who *do* love Him to give me money for the poor."

And so Amy prayed now that those who loved God would give her money for her mission hall. Almost miraculously Amy was invited to lunch with Kate Mitchell, an older and very wealthy matron. The butler served them lunch in a sunny room. To Amy, the older lady was a "white violet" in the sunshine. Amy explained, bolstered by the hope Christ can give, that the mill girls would certainly like to meet in their own hall. All they needed were the land and five hundred English pounds to build such a hall of sheet steel.

"Five hundred pounds?" The older lady blinked at the magnitude of Amy's request.

Yet, within days, Amy received a letter from Kate Mitchell. "Build your hall," she wrote. But Amy still needed property on which to build. She rushed to the office of a wealthy mill owner. "Can you not encourage the moral strengthening of the mill girls?" she argued. Had he known Amy's father? Or was he overcome by Christ? He virtually donated the property for the hall. Soon construction was begun on the grounds at Cambria Street. Some dubbed the hall the "tin tabernacle," but Amy named it "Welcome Hall." The grand opening was set for January 2, 1889, which she announced in printed cards with the simple invitation:

Come one, Come all,
To the Welcome Hall,
And come in your working clothes.[1]

Amy had secured an affiliation with the Young Women's Christian Association, known as the YWCA. For the opening of Welcome Hall, she hung a banner above the speakers' platform to the glory of the Lord: *THAT IN ALL*

THINGS HE MIGHT HAVE THE PREEMINENCE. They were
Saint Paul's words in his letter to the Colossians. Of course,
Amy, the "Nobody," was not on the speakers' platform. She
sat inconspicuously in the midst of her shawlies. But when
the real work began, once again she was front and center.

The first Wednesday of every month was their gospel
meeting. Every Sunday they had Bible class, followed by a
meeting of the Sunbeam Band. Monday was choir practice,
Tuesday was night school, Wednesday was girls' meeting,
and so on throughout the week. Not one day lacked activity.
With more than five hundred girls involved in the activities,
Amy needed to enlist many helpers. And more money was
needed. So the mill girls held bazaars in which they sold
their own handiwork. Amy's work was truly blessed now.
Some things happened that seemed miraculous. Once during a meeting she prayed for funds so that her mill girls
could all have a meal. A well-dressed man named Mr.
Buchanan came into the meeting and dropped a gold coin
on the table. She learned later that he was called "Sweetie"
Buchanan because he was a very wealthy candy manufac-
turer from Glasgow. Amy's Welcome Hall was now becoming known to Christians all over the British Isles. Letters
came, too. One in particular was startling.

"Mr. Jacob MacGill of Manchester has invited me to
come there to begin another 'Welcome Hall' for their mill
girls," Amy told her mother.

"Manchester? So far away. . ."

"That's not all, Mother. He wants you to come to su-
perintend a rescue mission for women."

"Me!"

So in 1889, the same year Amy opened her first Welcome Hall, she traveled to Manchester, a great factory city

in the west of England, to open another. The Welcome Hall in Belfast was left in the very deserving and capable hands of Kate Mitchell. In *Scraps,* Amy's brothers reported that she candidly predicted she would never be a wife. She was twenty-two years old, and it wasn't that she did not love men, but her love for men was *agape,* the Greek word for true Christian love, not physical love. In fact, Amy loved all people, men and women, with *agape.* Her *agape* was tested in Manchester, where she lived in the slums. Nighttime was the worst. Toughs fought in the streets. Women were molested. Hiding away in a room at night was no haven, either, because the rooms crawled with loathsome creatures of the night: roaches, ticks, bedbugs, rats.

"I do believe I could tolerate any place on earth now," speculated Amy, wondering how significant such a thought might prove. Was "going forth" always in the back of her mind?

Once, Amy walked late at night through the slum to the train station. She intended to take a train to Cheshire, where her mother had a cottage. Suddenly she was surrounded by young men, loud and smelling of rum. She was calm, fending them off as a gentle lady would. But the hooligans goaded each other on in their evil intentions. It was soon apparent that Amy might suffer the same fate as many other shawlies. She weighed less than one hundred pounds, and the thugs could easily wrestle her down in the dark street.

"Oh, God, don't let this terrible crime happen," Amy prayed, trembling.

"Stop!" A door suddenly opened, and a woman hurled herself into the mob. She grabbed Amy's hand and somehow the two muscled their way through the throng of young men. The woman shoved Amy inside her house and turned to face the mob. Amy heard the woman deliver a tongue-lashing; the words were indistinguishable, but the force was as violent as a storm. Whatever the brave woman said to the mob worked, and the hooligans were soon gone. Amy continued on to the train station in a daze. It was as if she had been rescued by one of Lot's mighty angels. And who could say the fierce woman was not an angel? In either case, the Lord was faithful.

As her mystical experiences increased, so did her humility. Why did she deserve such grace? At the Manchester Free Library, she read for the first time Dante's masterpiece, *The Divine Comedy.* When she discovered that the noble Beatrice was the love of Dante's life and his guide through Paradise, Amy wondered whether she should continue to use Beatrice as her middle name. She thought herself undeserving.

Norman and Ernest Carmichael, two of Amy's brothers, had emigrated to America; but Robert Wilson often invited Amy and her sisters and younger brothers to Broughton Grange, his majestic estate near Cockermouth, in Cumberland, above the River Derwent. No more than ten miles to the west, Solway Firth yawned into the Irish Sea. To the east ranged the Cumbrian Mountains. About twelve miles upriver, hugging the high lakes, was Keswick. The area reeked of history. William Wordsworth and Samuel Taylor Coleridge both had lived and had written poetry in this lake country. But as much as Amy loved poetry, she was more impressed by church history.

"Up at Keswick where we hold our meetings is where John Wesley set out on his desperate ride on September 27, 1749," explained Robert Wilson.

"Desperate ride?" his listeners asked raptly.

Robert Wilson explained that John Wesley had made

a pact with his brother Charles to share their matrimonial plans, but John was secretly planning to wed Grace Murray. Charles found out and confronted John about his betrayal. Afterward, Charles was so angry, he stormed off on horseback to find Grace Murray in Hinely Hill. When it finally dawned on John what Charles had done, he, too, set off from Keswick on horseback, impulsively—not methodically at all—as revealed by a copy of his journal in Robert Wilson's extensive library:

> *Wednesday 27th—I took horse at half an hour past three. There was no moon, or stars, but a thick mist; so that I could see neither road, nor any thing else; but I went as right as if it had been noonday. When I drew nigh Penruddock Moor, the mist vanished, the stars appeared, and the morning dawned; so I imagined all the danger was past; but when I was on the middle of the moor, the mist fell again on every side, and I quickly lost my way. I lifted up my heart. Immediately it cleared up, and I soon recovered the high road. On Alstone Moor I missed my way again; and what, I believe, no stranger has done lately, rode through all the bogs, without any stop, 'til I came to the vale, and thence to Hinely Hill. . . .*

"But Charles managed to prevent the marriage," added Robert Wilson.

Amy's desire to know more was kindled. Oh, how vast and intimate was Robert Wilson's knowledge of things! What passion! Imagine, of all people, John Wesley—perceived to be dry and orderly—riding madly across these very vales and hills, coattails flying, clutching his three-cornered hat. Just the fact that he rode like that thrilled Amy because she, too, loved to ride. Perhaps she had a wrong idea of what it meant to be religious. Subduing the self didn't mean removing all passion.

Amy went once again to the Keswick meetings as a guest of Robert Wilson, whom all the Carmichaels now referred to as "the D.O.M.," for "Dear Old Man." Never had he seemed more fatherly to her. Amy still wrestled with her thoughts of "going forth." In the flyleaf of her Bible, she recorded for "Keswick 1889":

> How great is His Goodness,
> and how great is His Beauty!
> Jesus I am resting resting,
> in the joy of what Thou art
> I am finding out the greatness
> Of Thy loving heart.[2]

Amy had taken Zechariah 9:17, "For how great is his goodness, and how great is his beauty!" and added her deepest belief that while she was resting, she was fathoming the Lord's greatness. Unsaid was her conviction that all this was in preparation for some future endeavor.

But what?

When she returned to Manchester, she became ill. Others—like her very good friends Ella Crossley and Mary Hatch—blamed her poor eating habits. As often as not, Amy made a meal of an orange or a tomato, while her eyes were locked on the pages of a book. There weren't enough hours in the day to do everything she wanted to do. And now she was sick. "Oh, you donkey!" Amy berated her wispy body. She did not regard her body as some regarded their bodies, as either a terrible prison of the soul or a thing of glory. No, Amy agreed with the saintly Francis of Assisi. Her body was like a donkey! Often it was sturdy and forbearing and lovable. But on the other hand, so often it was lazy and stubborn and exasperating!

"Oh, phooey on this donkey of mine!" Amy fumed.

Then came a development that stunned her.

In 1890, Robert Wilson asked Mrs. Carmichael if Amy could come to live with him at Broughton Grange. He would take her in as his own daughter. He had not only lost his only daughter, but he had also lost his wife. Broughton Grange was a lonely, unlovely place without the companionship and refinement of a lady. Could Amy come? Yes, agreed Mrs. Carmichael.

Mr. Wilson had been born a Quaker and the Friends' Meeting House was nearby. Built in 1653, it was not quite as old as the nearby Baptist Chapel. Wilson and his two bachelor sons, William and George, were quite active in both churches. Once, after reading the Bible intensely, Robert Wilson had determined that baptism was a righteous thing. And although Quakers did not baptize, he had himself baptized.

"We must drop labels," he said to Amy. "If our precious Lord came tomorrow, what use would we have of such labels?"

Amy had already begun to think similar thoughts. She had known Presbyterian ways from babyhood, but she had learned in Harrogate to appreciate the pious yearnings of Methodism. She had also learned to value the beautiful ritual of the Church of England. Now she would learn to enjoy the quietness of the Quakers and the earnest beliefs

of the Baptists. Surely these were all good things, all meant
to honor the Lord.

Robert Wilson instructed her like a father. "Be a deep
well, daughter," he told Amy.

He had become chairman of the Keswick Convention. Though he spoke with many people, he had learned
never to divulge privileged conversations or repeat gossip.
Amy was now privy to many of these same confidential
talks. She, too, had to be a deep well who knew much but
said little. Robert Wilson demonstrated a gentleman's sensitivity for everyone. Many times he plucked a flower for
Amy. He bought her a spirited pony to ride. He surprised
her with a pup. She named the frisky black-and-tan terrier
"Scamp."

But Amy was hardly a coquette or an idler. She had to
be busy for the Lord. She was active in the Children's Special
Service Mission in Broughton Grange. Tuesday nights at the
mission hall belonged to the children. Amy appeared like a
quiet force and soon ran the meetings. Although George
and William Wilson participated, it was often Amy who delivered the talks. And more and more children flocked in to
listen. She was so successful and the children were so demanding that Bible classes were added on Saturdays.

In 1890, Amy attended the Keswick meeting again,
this time recording in the flyleaf of her Bible:

> Thou hast put goodness in my heart.
> Thou will perfect that which concerneth me.
> Lord, let the glow of thy great love
> Through my whole being shine.[3]

Amy often combined her own compositions almost

seamlessly with verses from the Bible. Her own "Thou hast put goodness in my heart" she followed with "Thou will perfect that which concerneth me," from Psalm 138, inserting her own thought once again of being prepared for some future mission.

Her heart told her that this time at the Grange was a preparation for her "going forth." She was never idle. She reinforced her spiritual reading. She had a stable of favorite authors that she studied. Some were lesser known, like Brother Lawrence and Samuel Rutherford. To Amy, Rutherford, the seventeenth-century Scottish nonconformist, was very wise, very deep, a spiritual forerunner of her D.O.M. Others she read were widely known, like Thomas à Kempis and John Bunyan. Reading Bunyan's *The Pilgrim's Progress* was like reading the Bible. The eminent preacher Charles Spurgeon, whose sermons Amy's father had treasured, had said "scratch Bunyan anywhere and he bleeds Bible." How true it was. But Amy was fascinated by Bunyan's *Grace Abounding,* too. In his autobiography Bunyan detailed how God had revealed Himself. Once. Twice. Yet, for a long time, Bunyan refused to believe the "miraculous."

In fact, many of Amy's favorites had one thing in common: God had revealed Himself to the writer. It was no surprise that she was attracted to the writings of the "English Mystics"—a medieval group that included Raymond Lully, Lady Julian of Norwich, and Richard Rolle. How passionate was Rolle's love for God:

> *Oh beautiful Eternal Love that lifted us from the depths and revealed to us the wonder of your divine Magnificence. Come to me, my Love! I gave up everything I had for you. I spurned all that might*

have been mine, so my soul might house and comfort
you. Do not forsake me when you know I am burn-
ing with desire for you; when you know that my
most fervent desire is to be embraced by you. Grant
me grace to love you and find rest in you, so that in
your Kingdom I may see you forever. . . .

Amy also passionately desired His love, His revelation!
She read the mystical fire of Lady Julian of Norwich, too:

Our Lord uncovered my spiritual eye and it saw my
soul in the middle of my heart. It was as immense as a
whole kingdom. I understood it to be a splendid city,
with Lord Jesus, true God and true man, enthroned
in the middle. . . . He resides in the soul, in peace and
repose, to reign over all things on earth and in
heaven. . . . He will never abandon this place in our
soul, for in us He has a true home. . . .

Could Amy herself write with such passion? Her
friendship with the Faith Mission brought an invitation to
write an article for their magazine, *Bright Words*, but she
was reluctant. Amy was startled to hear the words, "I will
hold thy right hand!"[4] Had she actually heard God speak?
Was she going to be a doubter many times over like John
Bunyan? She recognized the allusion to Isaiah 41: "For I
the LORD thy God will hold thy right hand, saying unto
thee, Fear not; I will help thee." So Amy began writing
what she knew about: the shawlies. Her article, which she
titled "Fightin' Sall," chronicled the conversion of a shawlie
at the Welcome Hall in Belfast.

"Of course I realize now I must sign myself Amy *B.*

Carmichael. Dante's 'Beatrice' is much too grand for the likes of a 'Nobody.'"

But as contemplative and creative as Amy became, she remained very active in religious life, too. In 1891 she went with Hannah Govan of Faith Mission to evangelize along the Clyde River in Scotland. Amy's talks were well received. This approval among the Scots—who were known to be so taciturn that even John Wesley had thrown his hands up in despair—was surely a good sign. And she recorded in the fly-leaf of her Bible, on September 23, 1891—a hymn-singing Wednesday to be precise—one of the very special reminders:

And God is able to make all grace abound toward you; that ye, always having all sufficiency in all things, may abound to every good work.

Once again, Amy was strongly affected by John Bunyan, because the verse she records—2 Corinthians 9:8—offered both theme and title for his autobiography, *Grace Abounding*. And it was clear she intended to abound in good work, just as soon as God revealed His plan for her. Still, at Keswick that year she prayed for release from this constant inner tension about going forth to the heathen. Could not God give her some peace? Was it wrong for her to want to remain with Robert Wilson to comfort him? And could she have not only peace, God, but gladness also? Joy?

By January 1892, Amy had been at Broughton Grange nearly two years. Her piety had finally conquered the Wilson sons, George and William. At first resentful that this strange young woman had entered their lives, they now treated her like a younger sister. Amy had regarded their coolness as a trial for her. Though she seemed almost at peace now, it was true that joy was not there yet. But she was patient. And was it so bad in the manor, by the fire-place, with fields outside piled with snow?

As it happened, the evening of January 13 was any-thing but peaceful.

FIVE

The morning of January 14, 1892, a very shaken Amy wrote to her mother:

My precious Mother,

Have you given your child unreservedly to the Lord for whatever He wills? . . . Oh, may He strengthen you to say "Yes" to Him if He asks something which costs.

Darling Mother, for a long time as you know the thought of those dying in the dark—fifty thousand of them every day, while we at home live in the midst of blazing light—has been very present with me, and the longing to go to them, and tell them of Jesus, has been strong upon me. Everything, everything, seemed to be saying "Go," through all sounds the cry seemed to rise, "Come over and help us." Every bit of pleasure or work which has

49

*come to me, has had underlying it the thought
of these people who have never, never heard of
Jesus. . . .*

*But home claims seemed to say "Stay," and I
thought it was His Will; it was, perhaps, until yesterday. I can't explain it, but lately the need seems to
have come closer, and I wrote down a few days ago,
just to have it in black and white, why I am not
going.*

1. *Your need of me, my Mother.*
2. *The great loneliness it would mean to my dear
   second Father.*
3. *The thought that by staying I might make it
   easier for the others to go if He called.*
4. *My not being strong.*

*But. . .yesterday. . .I went to my room and just
asked the Lord what it all meant, what did He wish
me to do, and, Mother, as clearly as I ever heard you
speak, I heard Him say*

"GO YE"[1]

So there it was.

How the devil had planted good reasons for her not to
obey! But Amy was struck by the snowy fields outside the
windows. There was one worthy long ago who had fought
the lion on a snowy day. Benaiah, one of three mighty men
of King David, had "slew a lion in the midst of a pit in time
of snow"! And that was what Amy had done: slew the
devil—that "roaring lion" in the words of Saint Peter—in
time of snow!

Several days later Amy received her mother's answer:

Darling, when He asks you now to go away from within my reach, can I say nay? No, no, Amy; He is yours—you are His—to take you where He pleases and to use you as He pleases. I can trust you to Him, and I do. . . .[2]

Amy's sisters were confused. How could Amy go so far away? But Mrs. Bell, a Quaker friend of Mrs. Carmichael's who had so often understood Amy better than anyone else, clapped her hands in approval. It was Mrs. Bell who had silenced people when they badgered Amy about eating so little, saying, "The Lord takes care of such people." Some people around the Broughton Grange bluntly called her a selfish ingrate. But the D.O.M., Robert Wilson, the one person other than her mother who should have been hurt most by Amy's departure, wrote to Mrs. Carmichael:

It hardly seems a case for anything but bowing the head in thankful acquiescence, when the Lord speaks thus decidedly to one so dear. . . . She has been and is more than I can tell you to me, but not too sweet or too loving to present to Him Who gave Himself for us. . . .[3]

By the same post Amy admitted to her mother she didn't really know *where* she was going forth. Ceylon? China? Africa? Robert Wilson began to make discreet inquiries to various mission societies. It was hardly a surprise that China came into focus. After all, Hudson Taylor was a personal friend of Robert Wilson's. And Amy had actually met the great missionary to China. By May 1892, the D.O.M. had arranged for Amy to meet the Robert Stewarts in Bedford. The Stewarts were on leave from their mission in China. Ironically, the Stewarts were not missionaries of Taylor's China Inland Mission Society but of the Church of England's Church Missionary Society. Amy would represent a distaff society called the Zenana Mission Society. Again Amy was thrilled by the history of her surroundings; John Bunyan had written *The Pilgrim's Progress* in Bedford. Everything seemed most congenial with the Stewarts. They would return to their mission in the sea-coast province of Fukien in the autumn. Amy would be a welcome addition.

But July brought a disappointing letter to Amy back in Broughton Grange. "Oh, no. The Stewarts are not going directly to China. They are being detoured to Australia. . . ."

Suddenly Amy was the topic of discussion at the annual Keswick meeting. For several years they had saved funds to sponsor a missionary. Now Robert Wilson, who happened to be the chairman of the mission committee, pushed hard to make that first missionary none other than Amy Carmichael. Amy wrote in the flyleaf of her Bible: "Keswick, Tuesday, July 26, 1892: Day the Mission Committee met,"[4] then the telling passage from Psalm 47: "He shall choose our inheritance for us."

Robert Wilson's motion carried.

Present at the meeting was Hudson Taylor. So Amy was not surprised to find herself traveling in September to the China Inland Mission offices in London. The D.O.M. escorted her. Their hostess was Henrietta Soltau, who took charge of all women candidates for missionary work. To honor Robert Wilson, Amy signed the papers "Amy Wilson

Carmichael." After the D.O.M. left for Broughton Grange, Henrietta helped Amy settle into her room at one of their residences on Pyrland Road.

Suddenly Amy blurted, "Some people are saying that if I leave Robert Wilson, he will pine away and die. Under such dire circumstances, should I go?"

"Yes, even under such circumstances you should go." And Henrietta hugged Amy.

Geraldine Guinness, a thirty-year-old woman, also befriended Amy. Geraldine was well known in missionary circles. Her father and mother ran the East London Institute for Home and Foreign Missions, mercifully known as "Harley House." Geraldine was on leave from China, where she had labored since 1888. She was very bright and, like Amy, gifted at writing. It was rumored she would eventually marry Hudson Taylor's son, Howard. Amy and Geraldine had heart-to-heart conversations. Amy confessed her worry over leaving Robert Wilson. Geraldine had secret worries, too.

"Never weaken," whispered Geraldine once, and slipped a bit of folded paper into Amy's hand.

Back in her room, Amy read a message on the outside of the folded paper, "Love and deepest sympathy, my dear Amy, and many thanks for your precious helpful words yesterday."[5] Amy unfolded the paper. It read:

Can ye?
(MARK 10:38)
Can ye drink of the cup that I drink of— and be baptized with the baptism that I am baptized with?

Can God?
(PSALM 78:19; MARK 10:27)
Ye shall indeed. . . For with God all things are possible.

Now is my soul troubled; and what shall I say?
Father, save me. . .Father, glorify thy name. For
this cause came I unto this hour. (John 12:27–28)[6]

What a godly friend Amy had in Geraldine. And what was Geraldine's worry? Amy, "the deep well," never revealed it. But how at peace Amy now felt with her own future.

But then her peace was shattered.

"The doctor has not approved you for China," Henrietta Soltau told her.

"But how can that be?"

"My dear, we can't all be as strong as an ox."

Amy felt the world had fallen on her. Was her "going forth" destined to be like that of the great missionary pioneer, William Carey? Carey had been on his ship, waiting for the crew to draw anchor and cast off for India. Instead, he and his son were cast off the ship. Then he went through weeks of agony, sheepishly shrugging his bewilderment, wondering if he would ever go to India. Oh, the pain and shame for Christ. Would Amy prepare to leave and then return sheepishly to her loved ones again and again?

Back at Broughton Grange the D.O.M. was ecstatic. "God has given me back my Isaac!"

Yet Amy was restless in the extreme. This setback simply would not do. She would never rest until she went forth. God had commanded her. When Robert Wilson saw her continued resolve, he swallowed his joy and began to help her make contacts again. On January 13, 1893, precisely one year from her commission to go forth, she was struck by the thought that her destination was Japan. So the D.O.M. wrote Reverend Barclay Buxton, who ran a mission on the west coast of Japan. Buxton was a missionary for the Church

Missionary Society. However, he had in his organization missionaries of other less substantial societies, one of which was called the Japanese Evangelistic Band. When Wilson heard through Hudson Taylor that three missionary women of the China Inland Mission were sailing for Shanghai, Amy jumped at the opportunity to have travel companions. She was going to wait for Buxton's reply, not in Broughton Grange but in Shanghai!

No one could dissuade her.

On March 3, 1893, Amy sailed aboard the middling steamer SS *Valetta*. She did not have funds to travel the luxurious Peninsula & Oriental line, even in second class. She was drained. First, she had endured a tearful farewell in Manchester with mother and brothers and sisters. Then she had withstood an elaborate but emotional farewell in London with Hudson Taylor and other officials. Then at the port of Tilbury she had weathered another heartbreaking parting with Robert Wilson. To her dismay, as the ship cast off, Robert Wilson was able to stroll along the dock for half a mile, all the while reciting Scriptures that tore at her heart. They exchanged soul-wrenching hymns until Amy's throat was raw from tension. She was sensitive anyway. She could scarcely bear to see a butterfly falter. A lame sparrow buckled her knees.

"Never again do I want to suffer such an emotional gauntlet," she declared to herself.

She felt broken. But not too broken to record the date in her flyleaf and the phrase "He Goeth Before," alluding to John 10:4: "And when he putteth forth his own sheep, he goeth before them, and the sheep follow him: for they know his voice." She was compelled to make herself useful. She offered her services to the captain. He humored her by asking for a fresh Bible verse every day. She cheerfully obliged. But soon Amy was part of a Bible class with the other missionaries and a few passengers. One passenger she actually seemed to pull to Christ. Surely one soul was worth a thousand such trips, although she remembered not to credit the conversion to her one "hammer blow."

In the Mediterranean Sea, the ship was battered by a vicious storm. It seemed almost a test from God. She remembered reading John Wesley's journal entries about the storm he encountered at the age of thirty-two in the Atlantic. Fear petrified him, while German Moravians aboard ship with Wesley were in total peace. It was then he knew his faith in God was a sham. He had to rejuvenate his faith later. And what of Amy, age twenty-five? Some of her fellow passengers were trembling in terror.

"Yet I feel no fear whatever," she said in wonder.

She was at total peace! The freedom from fear made it seem a very fruitful voyage. Besides, there were few things Amy liked better than the companionship of other devout Christians. She marveled at that one-hundred-mile wonder, the Suez Canal. And who could not notice the peculiar transformation of the British passengers? At Port Said they all purchased sun helmets or "topees," the inexperienced travelers buying old-fashioned oversized pith helmets, the experienced travelers buying more fashionable head wear. No self-respecting Briton would be without a head covering in the tropics. Passengers laughed uproariously at the gully-gully man who came aboard to entertain them with magic tricks. But they were laughing at him, for Port Said seemed to mark the beginning of complete disdain for all dark skin.

In April, the SS *Valetta* sailed into the Indian Ocean

toward Ceylon. Nearly all voyages to the Far East stopped at this British colony.

"Land ho!" yelled one of the crewmen.

The distant horizon sprouted a dark bluish halo, which gradually transformed into a cap of green that grew into a lush landscape. They anchored in the harbor at Colombo, the capital city of the island of Ceylon. The English, who ruled that part of the world, talked as if there was no difference between Ceylon and its giant neighbor, India. But Amy was sure they were quite distinct. The people of Ceylon were predominantly Buddhists. The Indians were Hindus and to a lesser degree Muslims.

"At last the exotic East!" yelped one of the passengers as they disembarked.

Tall, swaying palms flagged the sky everywhere above a city that seemed a great garden. The air was hot and humid and heavy. The pungent odors of spices and sweat flooded Amy's nose. Shouting merchants, dinging bells, buzzing flies, and hammering shoemakers assaulted her ears. Movement was everywhere: people, pastries, sacks of grain. And such a kaleidoscope of colors: dark skins, ivory teeth, glittering jewelry, enameled boxes, combs, silks, brocades, merchants wrapped in various bright colors. Many of the men were half-naked with only their waists covered. The missionaries were whisked off in rickshaws pulled by men in harness, like draft animals. They rode to a mission where they were served breakfast.

Everyone at the mission made much of Keswick, and it seemed that many knew of the Keswick meetings. Amy was known as the "Keswick missionary." She was so emboldened, she played the organ and led the others in one of her favorite Keswick hymns. Inspired by the words of dying Samuel

Rutherford: "Glory, glory dwelleth in Immanuel's land," the hymn was called "The Sands of Time Are Sinking."

> *The sands of time are sinking,*
>   *the dawn of heaven breaks;*
> *the summer morn I've sighed for—*
>   *the fair, sweet morn awakes.*
> *Dark, dark hath been the midnight,*
>   *but day-spring is at hand,*
> *and glory, glory dwelleth*
>   *in Immanuel's land.*[7]

Amy next played another Keswick favorite, Frances Havergal's "Like a River Glorious" and its promise of Isaiah's "perfect peace." How relaxed Amy was. Yes, a life of trusting Christ did give perfect peace. The Lieschings, correspondents with the Carmichael family, were there in Colombo, too, to express the hope Amy would join their Heneratgoda Village Mission in Ceylon.

Another missionary said earnestly, "Perhaps the Lord will send you back again soon."

Somewhat startled by their interest, which seemed eerily prophetic, she boarded the *Sutlej*, a ship far inferior to the *Valetta*. Because Amy was not going on to India, Britain's "crown jewel," she had to change ships. The squalor aboard the *Sutlej* was no worse than the conditions she had suffered in Manchester. She conquered the insufferable smallness of her compartment by sleeping on deck. In the minute cabin she hung a piece of paper on which she had written Paul's "In every thing give thanks." As usual Amy offered her services to the captain. He was a troubled man, and to Amy's amazement, her conversations with him restored his faith and brought him to Christ.

"You not only live your faith," he said, "but I see Christ in you."

Again Amy reminded herself not to take credit for the one "hammer blow." Still, she instructed the captain and arrived in Shanghai with her heart singing. How many people were waiting for a witness? She urged the captain not to backslide and left with the other missionaries to go to the China Inland Mission. Awaiting her there was a letter from Barclay Buxton. He was ecstatic that she was joining him and his wife. They had recently lost several workers, and in their province they had to evangelize more than one thousand villages! Mr. Buxton assured Amy that he cared nothing about denominational differences, even quoting the Keswick motto: "All one in Christ Jesus."

The morning of April 25, 1893, on the steamer *Yokohama Maru*, Amy arrived in Shimonoseki, Japan. The Sea of Japan was known for its calmness, yet the steamer was caught in a storm in the Tsushima Strait and could not anchor in the harbor. Amy had to be lowered into a heaving tug to make it to shore. There a missionary from the Japanese Evangelical Band was supposed to pick her up. But all she encountered were gesticulating, chattering Japanese. What were they supposed to do with this young woman, so frail and pale? Amy could not help but laugh at the absurdity of her circumstances. Finally, an American was attracted to the frantic situation. He surmised that her contact had been waylaid by the storm and had a rickshaw take her to a local mission.

"It will all work out," said the American.

It was at the mission that Amy had an experience reminiscent of the great David Livingstone's when he first arrived at a mission in Africa: The various missionary societies were bickering with each other, and the missionaries squabbled among themselves. "All one in Christ" seemed a foreign concept to them. "Well, good heavens," said one woman indignantly to Amy, "you didn't think all missionaries love each other, did you?"

"Actually, I did," replied Amy.

Shimonoseki was the westernmost town on the island of Honshu, by far the largest island of Japan. Shimonoseki had more than one hundred thousand people. Nearby was the giant city of Hiroshima. Much of the island was mountainous, so the inhabitants crowded along the lowlands bordering the Sea of Japan. A seemingly endless series of small towns hugged the northern coast of Honshu, which stretched for 150 miles to Matsuye. One never seemed really away from a town, and in that way Japan seemed like southern England. The people cultivated rice and vegetables to eat with the bream and mackerel they netted from the sea.

Christianity had been introduced to Japan as early as 1549 by the Jesuit missionary Francis Xavier. At first, the Japanese feudal warlords—the shoguns—were receptive, allowing several hundred thousand Japanese to be converted from their peculiarly lifeless mix of Buddhism and Shintoism. But the shoguns soon became alarmed at the rapid conversions. By 1612, they looked the other way as Christians were massacred. By 1624, foreigners were not permitted to remain in Japan at all.

"By the second half of the nineteenth century," one missionary explained, "the pendulum had swung back the other way, and now Japan madly embraces Western traditions."

Feudalism had been replaced by a powerful emperor. Education, industry, the military, politics, and every other aspect of Japanese life seemed to be in the process of being Westernized. In 1872, primary education was mandated. By 1879, the university system was started for higher education. Christianity was allowed, but the tolerance was not easy to understand. Shintoism was the state religion, which emphasized worship of the divine emperor and the racial superiority of the Japanese. Was Christianity being tolerated only until the Japanese had modernized themselves? And why was Japan so anxious to modernize?

"They see what the Europeans and Britain have done with modern weapons," said one cynical missionary. "They see how these small Western countries have built colonial empires to enrich themselves."

"Yes," agreed another, "and the Japanese take Britain as their dearest model."

The current political system, with its Western-style cabinet, a prime minister, and a privy council, was an invention of the emperor and his advisors. The new constitution, based on extensive research in Europe and America, was initiated in 1889. Any resemblance to a democracy or a republic was an illusion. The emperor and his advisors were in complete control.

"Just as Britain prospers so mightily from her 'crown jewel,' India," said one of the missionaries, "so does Japan intend to prosper from a 'crown jewel' of her own."

"China," grumped someone, as if this conversation had occurred many times before.

"Oh, don't worry Amy so," said another. "The simple folks she will see in Matsuye know nothing of this empire building and all its intrigue."

"Yes, you'll have enough to do, young lady, to learn the language," said one.

Amy had to agree. All this speculation scarcely affected an English missionary or the average Japanese. And at the moment she had to learn the language. Long ago the Chinese taught the Japanese their method of writing by characters, or ideograms. Each Chinese character represented one particular word. Eventually the Japanese began using Chinese characters as phonetic symbols, each representing one syllable.

"That sounds very logical," said Amy in admiration.

The sounds of the Japanese language had only five vowels and nineteen consonants. Some sounds had no English equivalents. Their *r* was a result of flapping the tip of the tongue far forward in the mouth. Their *f,* produced with the lips not touching each other, was to Amy almost indistinguishable from their *h.* Some syllables were emphasized in Japanese by differing the pitch or tone, but the language was not a highly complex tonal language like Chinese.

"That's good to know," said Amy.

But the more she learned of the Japanese language, the more confounded she was by its complexity. Japanese vocabulary was very imprecise regarding the "visual." For example, the word *aoi* meant either "blue," "green," or "pale." On the other hand, Japanese was much more precise regarding sensations of hearing and touching. It seemed every circumstance had its own unique word.

"The word for rain falling varies according to what kind of surface it falls on!" said one missionary in an exasperated voice.

And then came the worst of all: Japanese grammar. The usual order of words in a sentence was subject, object, and verb. Modifiers usually preceded the words they modified. Nouns had neither gender nor number. No articles or prepositions, as known in the English language, were used. The verb had no number, no person, and no tense as understood by the British. Still, the use of the verb had to indicate whether or not the action was completed.

"It sounds so difficult," admitted Amy. "But surely, after I have a chance to practice, it will get easier."

SIX

A my arrived in Matsuye on May 1, 1893.

The town of about one hundred thousand people was buffered from the sea by a lagoon and an outer peninsula, although the gentle Sea of Japan was almost tideless anyway. Barclay Buxton and his family, though well intentioned, were unimpressed by Hudson Taylor's philosophy of missionary work and chose to live like colonialists. They resided in one of the town's largest houses, fully staffed by servants. The children had an English governess. They dressed in British clothing, and they ate potted meat and bread. They drank tea, but certainly not the weak Japanese variety.

"Must have proper tea," sniffed the Reverend Mr. Buxton.

When Amy first arrived and took up residence in the Buxtons' home, she, too, wore a proper English wardrobe. When the summer temperatures climbed into the nineties, she wore her cotton dresses. As fall approached and the air cooled, she wore warmer clothing like her blue serge dress. When the winter air had a bite in it, she added a light coat. And if January was especially bitter, her tweed coat and fur gloves were available.

Buxton had converted a Shinto temple into his Christian church. In spite of its promotion by the imperial government, Shintoism was not popular among the common Japanese. Buddhism was. But except for honoring the tradition of removing shoes, Buxton's church was undefiled by "foreignizing elements." But the charm of the Japanese way enthralled Amy. Their homes were all wood and paper with large sliding doors. Visible from all over the interior of the house was a spacious backyard, replete with dwarf trees, sparkling pools, and elaborate rock work. Cultivated all around Matsuye were trees of mulberry, cypress, yew, box, holly, myrtle, peach, pear, and orange. Above the town was a remnant of old feudal days: a walled castle of pagoda design in blues, greens, purples, and browns. The hills were forested with beeches, willows, chestnuts, and conifers. Matsuye was so beautiful, one was tempted to lead a life of contemplation.

"Go forth," Amy scolded herself one day.

She moved into another part of Matsuye to live with two other missionaries and began to venture out among the Japanese. She loved the Buxtons and regarded Barclay Buxton as a man of Christ, but she could not agree with his aloofness from the Japanese. She was enchanted by Japan. From the very first day, she wrote page after page of dialogue on thin rice paper for her family, occasionally intended for the newsletter they still called *Scraps*. Her letters were often adorned with exquisite drawings. Once, Amy sketched a kimonoed geisha girl strumming a stringed instrument like a guitar. The girl played only two notes but so gracefully it was mesmerizing. In many ways, Japanese customs proved the adage that less is more.

"But not so the elaborate complexity of their language," admitted Amy. "It so stumps my 'won't-work' brain I must resort to hiring an interpreter!"

The young woman Misaki San became her interpreter. Misaki was a Christian and very affectionate, but this use of an interpreter seemed a real defeat for Amy. She had been inspired by stories about how the great, irrepressible Dr. Livingstone had run off to isolate himself with the Africans until he was fluent in Bechuana. But, for some reason, hiring an interpreter seemed to Amy what God wanted her to do. One of the most difficult features of the Japanese vocabulary was the enormous number of respectful words—"honorifics" —indicating status. Their proper use was absolutely necessary. Misaki San guided Amy through the endless maze of honorifics.

To "go slowly" was in Japanese to "augustly leisurely go, deign to be." Occasionally, the convoluted politeness could be amusing. Once, on her rice paper, after describing a woman's silkworms, Amy began sketching them.

"You are deigning to do our honorable worms!" exclaimed the woman.

That summer her determination was tested. A man near her residence was said to be possessed by six "fox spirits." Amy had Misaki San take her to the man. The family resisted. They were strict Buddhists. They had no need of this Englishwoman's foreign superstition. Amy persisted. What was the harm? After all, the whole neighborhood had heard that the man was nearly dead. The man's wife agonized, then shrugged. She led Amy up a ladder to an attic room, where an old man was bound with cords to the crossbeams. Little mounds of powder smoldered on his chest, designed to drive off the spirits. Several had burned him badly. The Lord's words came to Amy, "In my name shall they cast out devils." The words could have been etched in stone. Amy felt enormous power.

She had Misaki San translate, "In the name of the Lord Jesus we will cast out the fox spirits!"

With that announcement, the man writhed and began to rage. He cursed and screamed and struggled to get loose. Oh, how he wanted to kill these intruders! This disturbed the man's wife and the other Japanese so much that they quickly ushered Amy and her interpreter downstairs. Amy was mortified. What had she done? Had she humiliated her Savior? But suddenly she was seized by courage.

Calmly she asked Misaki San to translate to the man's wife, "We are returning to our house to pray to our Lord Jesus, the Living God. Our God will conquer. Please let us know when the fox spirits are gone."

And pray Amy did.

One hour later, a man arrived at the house. With a smile that seemed a mile wide, Misaki San said, "He says the old man is well. The fox spirits are gone."

Hallelujah!

Amy had to contain herself:

I think I was taken to that upper room. . .to learn in such a way that I could never forget, that nothing was impossible to the God of the Impossible. . .[and when a man] was saved from the strong man's house, by a Stronger than he, my heart's word would always be Joseph's to the Pharaoh: "It is not of me." [1]

Amy CARMICHAEL

When Amy and Misaki San visited the house, the old man was tranquil. In complete control again, he presented Amy with a branch of pomegranate in flower. Did the old man know this orange-red was the hue of the fox? Perhaps not, but Japan seemed to flower for Amy now. Japan was a bouquet: blossoms of cherry, plum, azalea, peony, lotus, and yet to come were the chrysanthemums.

Because Amy had a substantial history with mill girls back in Ireland, she decided to approach the factory girls of Matsuye. Boys taunted her as she strolled the poorer part of Matsuye to invite girls to a meeting. "What is the foreign devil doing here?" jeered the youths. *Will the girls come?* wondered Amy. They toiled from five o'clock in the morning until six at night, with one day off every ten. To her astonishment, she drew eighty girls to a meeting! They were hungry for something different; she gave them Christ.

In August, Amy went up into the mountains. The missionaries were holding a consecration meeting at Mount Arima. Amy needed such a meeting. She had met a young Christian man who did not disguise his matrimonial interests in her. It was not the first time for Amy. After all, she was literate and perky and not homely at all. A few serious men had eyed her as a wife. But somehow she did not feel the need for a husband. She consoled herself with words of Thomas à Kempis: "True peace of heart can be found only by resisting the passions, not by yielding to them." At Arima she slipped inside a cave to pray for many hours. Years later she recalled:

> The devil kept on whispering, "It's all right now, but what about afterwards? You are going to be very lonely." And he painted pictures of loneliness—I can see them still. And I turned to my God in a kind of

*desperation and said, "Lord, what can I do? How
can I go on to the end?" And He said, "None of them
that trust in Me shall be desolate."*[2]

Newly consecrated, Amy returned to Matsuye determined to evangelize. She was more and more uncomfort-
able remaining so English. She began to eat more of the
Japanese food. At first it was repugnant to her. Much of
what they ate was raw fish; various, unidentified eggs; sea-
weed; sea slugs; and a very challenging-to-the-palate paste
of fish. Nevertheless, Amy persisted. It was not all alien.
Rice and chicken seemed dear old friends after eating a
slurry that reeked of too-ripe fish.

Her English clothing began to bother her, too. One late
fall day dawned unseasonably cold, and Amy wore her tweed
coat and fur gloves. That morning, through her translator,
Misaki San, Amy explained the Gospel to an old lady who
was very ill:

> *So I spoke and Misaki San translated, and our hearts
> prayed most earnestly. "Lord Jesus, help her. O help her
> to understand and open her heart to Thee now."*
>
> *She seemed to be just about to turn to Him in
> faith when she suddenly noticed my hands. . . . "What
> are these?" she asked, stretching out her hand and
> touching mine.*
>
> *She was old and ill and easily distracted. . . . I
> went home, took off my English clothes, put on my
> Japanese kimono, and never again, I trust, risked so
> very much for the sake of so little. . . .*[3]

The color of Amy's kimono was, of course, blue. The

elegant dress was trimmed in green, and down the left lapel she sewed in Japanese symbols "God is Love."

In November, the month of the chrysanthemums, she and Misaki San visited from house to house, a venture that steeled the nerves. One could never be sure of a warm reception. Once, an old lady stunned Amy by saying, "You have come here all alone, and we understand why very well."[4] It made Amy's heart sing; the old lady, so unreadable, suddenly revealed herself as a sage!

Another time, she and Misaki San virtually barged in on a man who was in his Buddhist devotions. Yet he was polite. After all, this honorable young woman was dressed as a Japanese. She was said to eat raw fish and sea slugs, too. But he was cautious.

"If what you say is true," he said to Amy after she presented the Good News, "then you are an angel from heaven to us. But that is all preaching. Can you show us you live in Christ?"

So there was the challenge for evangelizing: Could the evangelist show that she was living in Christ? She became less and less privileged, more and more like the common Japanese. She traveled in third class. She stayed in their hotels, sleeping on the floor in their communal bedrooms under blankets. This lifestyle obligated her to a great loss of privacy. Emboldened by her submission to their ways, many people on the street stared at her. They would even try to touch her. It was innocent enough. "No oil?" said one woman after testing Amy's hair. "Is that why it is so frizzy?" The Japanese loved to bathe communally, virtually boiling themselves in large tubs.

"That I refuse to do," Amy told Misaki San.

Each time before she left Matsuye, Amy prayed

fervently for the Lord to guide her. In November, she decided to visit the village of Hirose up in the nearby hills. On her first venture, she converted a young woman, a silk weaver. By this time, Amy had learned that converts in Japan were not ostracized as they were in some other countries. If a young woman was converted, she could still remain with her family. In December, Amy saved two more in Hirose. Two weeks later, four were saved, the last on Amy's twenty-sixth birthday, December 16, 1893.

In January 1894, Amy converted eight on a trip to Hirose. By this time, all the missionaries in Matsuye were praying with her. It had escaped no one's attention that, on each trip, the number of converts doubled. But the miraculous expansion soon ended. Perhaps the missionaries assumed too much. Or perhaps it was Amy's health. By January, she was suffering agonizing headaches. In fact, during the conversion of the eight, she wrote her mother, she could scarcely think from the pain. After she returned to Matsuye she was in bed for a week. Sometimes her eyes refused to see!

" 'Japanese head,' " pronounced Mr. Buxton.

"What is 'Japanese head'?" asked Amy in alarm.

"I don't think anyone really knows," he said in a puzzled voice, then added brightly, "but it's not permanent. That is, if you leave Japan."

"Leave Japan!"

"Don't be upset, Miss Carmichael. Perhaps it will go away on its own," he said unconvincingly.

Amy was depressed. She had given up on the Japanese language. She recorded with exasperation in her notes that the translation for the English expression "I like fine weather better than wet" was constructed in Japanese as "rain of coming down bad honorable weather than even good honorable weather of days of side good is."[5] How could she ever learn it? And now she had "Japanese head," a malady untreatable except by flight!

In May, Barclay Buxton suggested sending Amy to a China Inland Mission doctor in Shanghai. Perhaps the doctor there could help Amy. But Amy resisted. She had been in Japan only one year. A worried Mr. Buxton left Amy to her own devices when he departed Japan to take his family on leave. Almost immediately, Amy heard that the missionary in Imaichi was ill and needed assistance. She rushed to help. Imaichi was a village north of Tokyo on the other side of the great island of Honshu. Perhaps the different climate would improve her health. Amy decided to travel by ship. On board, a gust off the Pacific Ocean whipped the umbrella from her weak hands into the waves. She finally arrived in Imaichi but in worse shape than the missionary she had come to replace:

> On Sunday I collapsed. . .a terrible comedown, for I
> always declared nothing could make me faint. . . .
> But this time over I went and before I came back all
> the humiliating attentions attendant upon such de-
> partures had been showered upon me. . .and I find
> myself environed by wet towels, doleful faces, and a
> general sense of blurs. . . . This Imaichi work ended
> Japan for me. . . .[6]

When she was well enough again to travel, she returned to Matsuye, aware that now she must go to China. She had the joy of attending the baptism of some of her converts before she left. But that entailed posing in a photograph with them, which she hated because she did not like her own image. Her dislike seemed almost pathological, but it was a manifestation not of vanity but humility. How could she subdue the self while posing vainly for pictures?

"Must I be embalmed in this way?" she grumbled to herself but pursed her lips into a weak smile for the photographer. After all, this was something her converts wanted. No one needed to know that later on she would scratch her image out of her copy of the photograph! Nor did they know their catechist had a splitting headache. She did indeed need a change of scene.

In the meantime, she lamented her outcome in Japan:

WILL NOT THE END EXPLAIN

The crossed endeavour, earnest purpose foiled,
  The strange bewilderment of good work spoiled,
The clinging weariness, the inward strain,
  Will not the End explain?[7]

In July, she bought a round-trip ticket and sailed for Shanghai. The parting was painful. Everyone pretended she would be back in six weeks. But who believed it? Amy felt as tragically temporary as a butterfly. On board, she opened a note from Misaki San. "I know you will miss me," Misaki San wrote bluntly, "but Christ is sitting by you now, so please talk with Him to forget me."[8] It was a brave note, but Amy knew that Misaki loved her like a sister and never wanted her to forget her.

The doctor in Shanghai recommended that Amy go to Chefoo in northeast China. His reason was that Chefoo was not only cooler but had a dry winter. But suitable accommodations at Chefoo didn't materialize. Meanwhile, Amy had an overwhelming desire to go to Ceylon! Was such a detour possible? She prayed that this was not God's will. People would think her erratic wanderings those of a madwoman. She went to the senior missionary in Shanghai, William Cooper. He did not discourage her at all but prayed with her. But her doubts remained.

> *What will people say? How strange it will look! Nobody will understand. And then home thoughts that I cannot write down—fears as to unsettlement of all your minds. Then like a swarm of mosquitoes the unkind misjudging remarks that many would make, and then, hardest of all, again and again fears about those nearest and dearest. Through them all came calmingly the assurance that, as to what hurt most, He would take care of that, and as to other, one must be content to be misjudged.*[9]

Amy wrote to a very young missionary friend at the mission the Lieschings ran in Ceylon. In the meantime, she discovered that passage to Ceylon was actually cheaper than traveling to Chefoo. That startling fact was a great relief to her. At least the trip didn't seem so crazy. Psalm 77:19 expressed her feeling so perfectly that she wrote it in the flyleaf of her Bible: "Thy way is in the sea, and thy path in the great waters, and thy footsteps are not known." She wouldn't wait for a response. On July 28, she was aboard ship and on her way to Ceylon.

"And only heaven is sweeter than to walk with Christ at midnight over moonless seas,"[10] she wrote in her Bible.

Her health was still shaky. Battling a fever, she arrived in Colombo on August 17. Her young friend was there to meet her. Amy found to her utter amazement that the

Lieschings had both succumbed to malaria. They were dead! The three rudderless young women remaining in the mission prayed fervently for help. The date they had beseeched God for a leader was July 14.

Amy gasped, "Why, I had my overpowering urge to go to Ceylon just after that!"

Though as a green missionary she scarcely regarded herself as a leader, Amy went happily to the mission, pushing aside the worry that she was not likely to recover her health in a malarial jungle. Ceylon was ancient like Japan but less populated. Although local cultivation had driven elephants and tigers back into the deeper jungle, leopards had a nasty habit of adapting to civilization. Snakes, too, stubbornly abounded. Amy chose to see the rose among the thorns:

> There, in the bright sunshine like a bit of blue flame among white flowers, the tiny chirping thing [a hummingbird] flitted to and fro. Now poising itself on a spray of shining blossom, diving its curved beak deep into each fragrant flower, never marring a petal, now fluttering in and out of the bush on which they grow, its clear electric tinting showing well against the green, and now for a moment motionless, half hidden in the whiteness, a little living jewel in a snowdrift of white flowers. . . .[11]

The Ceylonese people near the mission practiced Buddhism and spoke Sinhalese. The three young missionary women were of a mixed descent called "Burgher." Their ancestors were both Dutch and Ceylonese. Of course, the young women were perfectly fluent in Sinhalese. The tenor of their lives was revealed to Amy one day when a man barged into the mission house. He was the husband of a woman who had recently been converted. He waved a murderous-looking machete. Two of the young women knelt on the floor, closed their eyes, and prayed. Amy followed suit. What faith! At last she could not resist. She had to steal a glance. There he still stood—with the machete overhead!

She squeezed her eyes closed and implored God, *"Be merciful unto me, O God, be merciful unto me: for my soul trusteth in thee: yea, in the shadow of thy wings will I make my refuge, until these calamities be overpast."*

When Amy next looked up, the man was gone!

Only Christ gave her the courage to seek out such volatile people:

> *You go to a hut and find nobody in, you go to the next and find nobody wants you, you go to the next and find an old woman who says yes, you may talk if you like, and she listens in an aimless sort of way and perhaps one or two more drift in, and you go on, a prayer behind each sentence. . .sometimes, just when you think you have got a bit of the glorious Truth wedged in, when the heart seems touched by the wonderful story of Calvary, some little triviality comes up, and some question about pigs or eggs sends you back to the very beginning. But there are bright bits, too, times when a flash of Heaven's own sunshine lights up the darkness of the darkest mud hut, and one such moment is worth a lifetime's plod. . . .[12]*

Letters from outside unsettled her. First, there were letters from Misaki San, whose courage had broken down.

How she missed Amy! It was heartbreaking to read her letters. Then there was a letter from Barclay Buxton. Imagine his shock to hear that Amy had left Japan while he was on leave! "What a void you left!" he lamented. Mr. Buxton's consternation paled in comparison to the sentiments expressed in a letter she received from Robert Wilson. He was much disturbed by Amy's detour to Ceylon. After all, she was a missionary of the Keswick Mission Committee. He warned her not to officially join any mission house. This upset Amy more than anything. And she wrote him and her mother again that this effort in Ceylon was of Him. She had only followed His calling.

When Amy learned that Eva—her closest sister—was preparing to be a missionary in South Africa, she thought aloud, "Have her practice balancing herself on a pinpoint. It will be most useful!"

She wrote that very advice to Eva.

In all the muddle of activity—some upsetting, some uplifting—Amy had scarcely noticed how much her health had improved. But hadn't she been "Sent of the King" as she recorded in the flyleaf of her Bible? She saw a doctor. He warned her that under no circumstances should she try to return to Japan. She had just about resolved to write Matsuye to request that the rest of her belongings be sent to Heneratgoda, although it broke her heart to think of how Misaki San would receive the news. Perhaps the D.O.M. didn't want her to officially attach herself with this mission, but Amy was quite pleased with Ceylon. Even the Sinhalese language was coming to her. Surely the Lord wanted her there.

So the letter that she received November 27, 1894, hit her very hard.

SEVEN

Robert Wilson had suffered a stroke!

Within an hour of receiving the news, Amy had explained to her friends at the mission what had happened and had departed for Colombo. On December 15, 1894, the day before her twenty-seventh birthday, Amy was met by her mother in London. By December 21, she was at Broughton Grange comforting the D.O.M., who by now was almost seventy years old. Already he was recovering, but Amy had no regrets about her hasty return. She would stay with him at Broughton Grange.

"You must write about your experiences," urged the D.O.M.

"Oh, but I have. I've written letters home, some in the form of the newsletter *Scraps*. I've written letters to the Keswick magazine, too."

But soon she was synthesizing it all into a book. She even had her own line drawings for it. Robert Wilson's son

William added some appropriate sketches of his own. Would anyone be interested? Yes, after several months it was accepted for publication by the Marshall Brothers of London. The title would be *From Sunrise Land*, the intent a prayer for the heathen of Japan. Amy did little else that winter, except attend to Robert Wilson and ponder her future. In Japan she had failed as a missionary on two fronts. Her health was too fragile, and her facility for the language was lacking. But her stay in Ceylon had given her new hope. Perhaps there were places she could stay without being sickly. Perhaps there were languages she could master.

A letter from a friend in Bangalore, India, intrigued her—especially because the friend was a sister at the Church of England's Zenana Hospital and knew medicine. Amy noted:

> *She said the climate was healthy, delightful, in fact;*
> *it might be possible to live there even if China and*
> *Japan and the tropics were taboo. . . .[1]*

It pleased her mother, Robert Wilson, and all the other Carmichaels and Wilsons, too, for they had sensed that Amy was determined to "go forth" again. At least the locale in India appeared to be a congenial place. The British maintained a huge presence in India. And the climate seemed the kind that would not destroy Amy's health. So Amy agreed, although this time she received no specific "call" from the Lord. Bangalore was simply a convenient place to go.

For the first time in a very long time, Amy remembered that the dear Reverend Mr. Beatty of Millisle had a brother who had been a missionary to India. During one of the missionary's furloughs, he and his wife lived near the Carmichaels in Millisle. On Sunday afternoons, the wife regaled neighborhood children with stories of India. Amy—a young child at the time—was so fired by them that she didn't want to leave the woman's side. She didn't want the stories to end. But her childhood was so rich, and the stories had become lost in her great treasury of stories. "Now to think: I might be going to India."

As usual, Robert Wilson, the D.O.M., could facilitate almost anything. In May, Amy was given an interview in London with the Church of England's Zenana Mission Society. By July 26, they had notified the Keswick Mission Committee that Amy was accepted for duty in Bangalore. At a meeting the next day in the large tent at Keswick, Amy expressed her gratitude and said her farewells. She sprang the unexpected by unfurling a banner with golden words on a field of blue: "Nothing is too precious for Jesus."[2]

Her departure was yet several months off. In the meantime, whether she liked it or not, she was instructed in the ways of India. Because it was Britain's crown jewel, it seemed everyone had an opinion of India, even though its immensity defied generalities. In size, it was twenty times greater than the British Isles. The land teemed with mountains, jungles, plateaus, yawning rivers, and arid deserts. India's population —an estimated three hundred million inhabitants—was ten times greater than Great Britain's. The subcontinent was home to many languages and religions. The suffering in India was overwhelming. Several men sought to explain Indian politics to Amy. Britain, the great world power, had controlled India since the 1600s, over the centuries steadily increasing their influence. But in 1885, educated Hindus organized a nationalist movement, embodied in the Indian National Congress. Intrigue increased. Even now, the British were encouraging the formation of a Muslim League. This, reasoned the devious British, would split the native effort into bickering between Hindus and Muslims.

"Before long they will be fighting each other instead of Britain," offered one man with a shrug.

Another informant seemed just as depressing. "British India is made up of more than 560 native states. Each native state is ruled by a prince or 'maharajah,' who has absolute power within his own state. In return for stupendous wealth and power within his own state, the maharajah pledges support for Britain in time of war. And he also allows the British government at New Delhi to control all interstate and international relations."

Then dreadful news swept the Keswick community. The Robert Stewarts, whom Amy was going to accompany to the province of Fukien back in 1892, had all been murdered in that very province! That saddened everyone and reminded most of all her mother and Robert Wilson just how dangerous Amy's missionary work was.

But on October 11, 1895, she once again endured the heartbreaking good-byes and sailed for the East. Aboard a mediocre steamer in second class, she again noticed the peculiar transformation of the British passengers at Port Said. Because she was traveling this time to India, where class distinctions were deeply ingrained in the culture, the other passengers sought to "educate" her.

"You are most fortunate, Miss Carmichael," said one male passenger, "that you are arriving in India in 'cold weather.' That's when we party for several months."

"Oh, I don't think I'll be doing that."

"So much the pity then," sniffed the man, snapping his fingers at a waiter. "Boy! *Billyatapani! Burra peg!*"

Amy discovered that this imperious command was for three fingers of whiskey with soda water. Apparently social drinking in India had regressed from genteel clarets and brandies to head-numbing whiskey, gin, and cocktails. She prayed she would see little of that where she was going. Nor did she want to experience their frantic social calendar they called "cold weather." As she heard more and more talk, she realized that their claims of partying for several months were not too much exaggerated. On numerous occasions, the British assembled to party day after day. "We had a bashing good party every day for fourteen days during Rawalpindi," bragged one red-faced passenger over his gin.

"Just who are the heathens in India?" Amy asked herself.

Her destination was Madras, a port on the southeast coast of India. From there she would travel about 150 miles west into the highlands to reach Bangalore. Bangalore rested on the Mysore Plateau at an elevation of three thousand feet. The great city of more than one million inhabitants was known for its mild, dry climate. To grasp the enormity of India, Amy had only to remember that Bangalore was more than nine hundred miles from Calcutta to the northeast and nearly twelve hundred miles from Delhi to the north. On November 8, the ship anchored at Madras, and she disembarked. Naked poverty raged. Families were living on the streets, the better-off ones lying on mats made of palm leaves instead of the bare dirt. Virtually naked, many of these natives nevertheless wore bracelets and anklets with rings dangling from their noses and ears.

An Englishman near Amy saw her gaping. "The cities of India are like this," he explained. "These poor wretches flood in from the countryside looking for a better life. Thousands of them die on the street."

"This is our crown jewel?" blurted Amy. "What have we done?"

"I say, madam," he countered, "that's not fair. Look at the magnificent buildings we've put up here to show the superiority of our ways."

Madras had once been the focus of British power. Enormous Italianate buildings displayed massive columns and arches near the harbor. Although British power had shifted mainly to Calcutta, Bombay, and Delhi, Madras was still very important for the administration of southern India. Amy discovered that the story of maharajahs who administered the more than five hundred native states was a half-truth. Much of India had been annexed by the British outright. Although her destination, Bangalore, was in one of the native states, the entire eastern half of southern India was ruled by the British through subdivisions called "districts."

Amy soon learned that all European men were called *sahibs*, all European women were *memsahibs*. In every instance, native Indians deferred to a sahib or a memsahib. If a sahib or memsahib wanted something at a shop, the shopkeeper would abandon a native customer without hesitation. "Memsahib!" he would say, giving the palms-together salute of respect. Even on a crowded street, a native had better not brush against a sahib or memsahib. European travelers were whisked to a hotel and offered curried chicken and rice. Not so with an Indian. A native Indian was insane to think he might ever dine in English clubs or ride a horse on their polo greens.

"How profoundly depressing," said Amy, startling her informant. "And where is the Church Mission Society located?"

From Madras, Amy should have taken a train west to

Bangalore. But the Church Mission Society official in Madras, Mr. Arden, asked if Amy would stay with his daughter Mary while he visited an outstation at Ootacamund—which they all called "Ooty"—with his other daughter, Maud. Of course, Amy agreed.

November was the rainiest month of the year in Madras, with many drenching downpours. Still, she was assured, the temperature reached only about eighty-five degrees in the afternoon, compared to one hundred degrees in the summer; and in December, the monsoon rain abruptly tapered off—just in time for all the parties. In the week or so before Mr. Arden and Maud left, Amy learned much more about India.

"Don't you know the apostle Thomas came to India right after the Resurrection?" chirped the daughters. "He may have gone to China, too, but he returned to India before he died. He was martyred at Malabar. He is buried at Mylapore just outside Madras."

The daughters pointed out the very spot south of the Aydras River. The thought of one of the Lord's disciples—even his cast-off shell—being so nearby was stunning. India was so rich in history. Of course, Amy had experienced such feelings before. She had been impressed by realizing a worthy like John Wesley had done this or done that in a certain place she was standing on. But Thomas of the Twelve? It made her head swim with delight! Yet she remained very proper with the daughters.

The daughters were not ignorant about later Christianity in India. "Christians arrived at Kerala from Syria in the sixth century. At Kerala the Christians even retain a Syriac order of service. Of course in 1542, Francis Xavier, the Jesuit from Portugal, arrived at Goa. Protestants quickly followed suit. Both the Dutch and English established themselves in the Bengal area by the early 1600s. Of course you know all about the Baptist missionary William Carey, who worked near Calcutta and translated the Bible tirelessly into every language of India. . . ."

The daughters also breezily discussed the religion of the Hindus. "Their behavior is far simpler than their beliefs," said one. "They don't eat meat, especially their sacred cows, although they do eat eggs and fish. And they marry within their own caste. Probably few of them actually understand the complexities of their religion."

"Their caste system is very old," volunteered the other. "Originally there were four main castes—with another group of people excluded completely: the 'Untouchables.'"

"Oh, the system is so insidious," cried one of the daughters. "They believe in being reincarnated as another life form. The catch is that one can be reborn into a higher caste only if one stays strictly within that caste in this life. So you see it is very hard to get a Hindu to 'break' a caste. They are gambling with their souls."

"And the castes have been subdivided and subdivided until now there are thousands of castes," cried the other. "Yet there seems no hope for the Untouchables."

Except the hope of Christ, thought Amy.

Finally one of the daughters said reproachfully, "You have been here for a week, and you haven't said one word about the Lord Jesus Christ."[3]

Amy was flooded with shame. Later she wrote:

It was true I had not said one word. The girls were like butterflies, pretty and dressy, and I had been shy of them both. I had no idea they cared for the things

*of Christ and had thought I should wait until I
knew them better before speaking of these things. . . .
The friend who had led them to Christ had said I
would be coming by the next boat and that I would
help them. So all the time I had been thinking of
them as pretty butterflies they were really hungry
lambs. . .[oh,] the shame of that hour. But we have a
forgiving Lord. He gave us a wonderful time together. We rode together, read together, prayed together. We became fast friends. . . .*[4]

The first week in December, Amy was aboard a train
rumbling west into the highlands. Rice paddies were replaced by fields of millet carved into tropical forests. Usually
the countryside was peopled only in rough huts or drab
mud-brick buildings. But Hindu temples of all sizes were a
frequent sight. Muslim mosques, flagged by their distinc-
tive Byzantine minarets, could be seen less often. Rarest of
all was the sight of an enormous palace, so Italian she could
have been in Rome. Was that the way of all India? The few
very rich and the many very poor? At Bangalore Amy's
train was met by the friend who had written her about the
healthful climate. Almost immediately Amy was confined
to bed with a raging fever.

"Oh, my bones ache so," she told the doctor at the mission hospital.

"That's Madras for you," he said sourly. "You've picked
up dengue fever."

No! Dengue fever was also known as "breakbone" fever.
Amy now knew why. She ached everywhere. The only good
thing about dengue fever was that the severe pain ran its
course in one week. However, several weeks were required

to fully recover. It was during this recovery period that Amy had her twenty-eighth birthday. She was lying in a lounge chair by an open window. No one knew it was her birthday, yet suddenly a garland of flowers flew through the window to land on her lap.

"Why did you do that?" she called out the window.

"I don't know," answered the puzzled thrower.

Amy was quickly discovering that these Bangalore missionaries were the "verandah" type that the great Dr. Livingstone had held in such low regard. They spent a great deal of time enjoying the status of being British colonials. They hired natives—usually Muslims—to teach in their schools instead of mastering the languages and delivering the Good News themselves. They sat about, prattling and complaining and speculating. "Would these natives ever do anything for us if we didn't pay them?" queried one missionary cynically. No one disagreed, and no one offered a solution. In Japan, Amy had mulled over the question of whether Mr. Buxton of Matsuye was too much in love with British ways to be a good missionary, but Barclay Buxton was far superior to these missionaries in Bangalore. At least he had mastered Japanese so he could deliver the Good News.

The missionaries in Bangalore often gossiped about a missionary named Thomas Walker. He was a bit of a renegade, working far to the south, down in the hot lowlands of Tinnevelly. "I heard he's about ready to resign," said one missionary with relish.

"Oh, he won't resign," said another. "That's just his way of getting attention."

Yet the missionaries quoted Mr. Walker so often that Amy concluded that they really respected him. Amy tried to fathom this Thomas Walker. He sounded like a scholarly but very opinionated old person, who was cranky besides.

One of the other young women at the Bangalore mission came to Amy because she had heard that Amy wrote articles for mission magazines. The young woman said, "I sent a story to our mission magazine in England about a young Muslim girl who very much wanted to convert, but her parents prevented it. They wrote back that the ending was too discouraging. Should I invent a happy ending?"

"Heavens, no, you mustn't change the truth to please anyone!"

This righteous attitude did not endear Amy to some of the other missionaries. And they let her know it. But Amy accepted the hostility as whittling away at her self, a process she welcomed. And no complacency among others was going to keep her from serving Christ. As much as Amy had loved Misaki San, this time she was determined to remove the language barrier between herself and the local people. This zeal found her a vocation; she would be the one missionary at the hospital who spoke Tamil, one of two common languages in the province of Mysore. *Tamil will prove more valuable,* thought Amy, *because the other language, Cannarese, is more provincial.* Tamil was some kind of ancient, classical language for southern India, similar to the way that Latin formed the foundation for the European Romance languages. If Amy could master Tamil, she reasoned, she could make herself understood throughout southern India, even northernmost Ceylon. Perhaps it would also ease the learning of other southern Indian languages. She tried to ignore the raised eyebrows of other missionaries when Tamil was mentioned; apparently it was *the* most difficult language on the Indian subcontinent!

"They say it's worse than Chinese," gasped one skeptic.

Still, Amy began to study Tamil six hours a day. The hospital even provided her regular lessons with a native language teacher, called a *moonshee*. It was a comfort when she first realized Tamil's symbols—in fact, all the languages of India— were written horizontally from left to right, like English. Words were separated from each other by a space, too.

But the alphabet!

"It is rather different from what I'm used to seeing," she volunteered lamely to her moonshee.

"Ah! You see Tamil was originally incised into palm leaves with a stylus." He noticed her blank look. "In contrast to the northern languages of India that are written on paper with ink."

"Well, actually, I meant it is different from the English alphabet. How many vowels are there?"

"Only twelve."

"So many?"

"You see the Tamil alphabet is phonetic. Long and short sounds then must have their symbols. Yes, you have more letters to learn, but once you master the sounds of the alphabet, you master the sound of any word in Tamil." He added wryly, "Unlike English."

"How many consonants are there?" she went on doggedly.

"Consonants and vowel-consonant combinations," he corrected. "Only thirty-two."

"So I must learn forty-eight symbols in all?"

"Well, there are some sounds of the alphabet that require more than one symbol."

So Amy attacked Tamil. Some variations in Tamil were obvious, even pleasing. For example, the long and short *a*'s differed only by an added squiggle, as did the two *o*'s. But the two *i*s were completely different. And symbols for some sounds were exasperating. *Kau* required three symbols. And learning the alphabet was only the first step. She knew no vocabulary, no grammar. Still, she had once experienced something mystical with the Sinhalese spoken in Ceylon. She had prayed fervently for help, and the Sinhalese symbols that looked like so many worm tracks within a very short time became an alphabet.

"Oh, Lord, please help me with this Tamil language," she prayed. "With Your help I can do anything."

Such a severe regimen demanded a release of tension. Even though Bangalore had a rather peculiar two seasons of rain, in summer and fall, the rainfall was much less than along the coast, and the temperatures were much milder. There were only a few days when outdoor activity was marred by the weather.

Amy liked few things better than riding a pony at breakneck speed. She always started out with good intentions, riding sidesaddle. She sat in the saddle primly, her right leg hooked over the pommel of the saddle, her left foot in a stirrup, skirt modestly covering her legs. Because she could not squeeze the sides of the pony to increase her speed, she carried the customary whip for riding sidesaddle. Well, Amy detested the use of a whip. So who could blame her—after a few minutes of "walking" the pony—for swinging her right leg into the other stirrup and gently kneeing the pony in the sides to attain a trot. And if a trot, why not a canter? And if a canter, why not a gallop?

"Do you think it wise, Miss Carmichael," asked one of the missionaries at dinner one evening, "to race the carriage of the chief British official in Bangalore?"

"Was that the carriage of the Resident?" asked Amy, not

particularly disturbed by her action. "Is his nose out of joint?"

"How disrespectful," said another missionary, almost hysterical. "Don't you think the Resident has enough to worry about with the development of the new gold fields at Kolar?"

"Amy is Irish," explained another missionary.

The attitude of some missionaries that they were in India to protect British interests disturbed Amy very much. But she had to admit she herself did not feel very British. She never had. She didn't feel particularly Irish, either. Not even Scottish. She was, in the haunting words of Moses, "a stranger in a strange land," no matter where she went. Her only true home was sometime in the future: with God. As she learned more and more of the British rule of India, she became certain the British also had a caste system. It was impossible to miss. At the highest level were the government officials—and their wives, of course. At the next level were the professional Army officers. Below them were the businessmen. And at the lowest rung were the common soldiers. And where were the missionaries?

"We are the 'Untouchables,' " confided one not-very-discreet missionary. "Most British don't want us here. We interfere too much with their very pleasant lives."

Not enough, thought Amy.

A letter from Keswick cautioned her not to "cool." "Look to Him to keep you burning and shining."[5] Her old friend from Manchester, Ella Crossley, visited her early in 1896 and gushed over how well Amy spoke Tamil. But Amy was unhappy with her comfort—yes, even her wild pony rides—in Bangalore. The atmosphere was far too congenial. Once again she had spurned a marriage proposal. And the sad truth was that the large staff of missionaries were converting almost no one! When she got a chance to go out to Ooty for a meeting of people from the field missions, she jumped at it.

It was there she finally met Thomas Walker of Tinnevelly. His wife was there, too, a very pleasant woman.

Mr. Walker himself, however, was not very pleasant.

EIGHT

Thomas Walker was not much older than thirty-five, with jet black hair. He was so fiercely concentrated and humorless he seemed tedious to Amy. He was going to speak at the meeting, and she was glad she had brought her Tamil language books with her. His talk would probably be insufferably dull. But it wasn't. She thanked him afterward.

"I see you're studying Tamil," he said, glaring at the books in her hands.

"Yes," she cried enthusiastically, "and I long for the chance to live among the natives—in a mud hut preferably—and to learn the language directly from their lips." She almost added "just as David Livingstone did in South Africa," but surely Mr. Walker already understood all that.

"That method won't work at all," he said brusquely.

Well, of all the narrow-minded people! Was he a righteous man or a boor? *Oh, self, die,* she quickly corrected herself. It was the "me, me, me" in Amy that was stung by Thomas Walker. Nothing of any importance.

"I suppose you know a better way?" she asked, trying to smile.

"Yes, I do, young lady. You must come out to Tinnevelly, where Tamil is the first language of the natives, but not to live in a hut! I will personally instruct you."

She didn't answer. What was she to think? Confused, she went off by herself and sat under a great tree. She mustn't waste time brooding. Faith, hope, and love. God is all. For a long time she had been practicing the simple mysticism of Brother Lawrence as revealed in his tiny classic, *The Practice of the Presence of God*. Dying to self was from Brother Lawrence. *If one tried always to please God, one would know God's will*, she reminded herself.

"But I also know from Brother Lawrence that I must continue to work and not wait in idleness for answers."

Amy opened her Tamil grammar book. Suddenly she felt a presence, a listener. It was He. Amy realized she was to listen *with* Him. *"The voice of thy brother's blood crieth unto me from the ground"* was what came into Amy's mind as she listened. The book of Hebrews had expanded on that ancient cry from Genesis: "And to Jesus the mediator of the new covenant, and to the blood of sprinkling, that speaketh better things than that of Abel. See that ye refuse not him that speaketh." Time seemed to stop for Amy. Yet when she finally arose, she realized she had been sitting under the tree for hours.

"Here in Ooty I'm not in the real India at all," she murmured.

Every Indian in Ooty served a European. The truth was that Ooty itself was very British. One would never have known that in India the British were outnumbered one thousand to one by the native Indians or even that the sacred cows numbered tens of millions. With Simla, Darjeeling, Muree, and Naini Tal, Ooty was one of the acceptable "hot weather" retreats. Every place she had been, in fact, was insufferably British. Ooty was so British that "the right sort of people" assembled regularly to "ride to the hounds." Yes, they even maintained a pack of the very finest foxhounds, imported from England. Their quarry was a jackal, which served well enough as a substitute for a fox. And Amy had stumbled onto one party after a "birding." The two dozen hunters, including so-called ladies, were assembled for their photograph with hundreds and hundreds of dead sand grouse laid in rows. The organizers had even printed a program with the scores of the participants. One British gentleman had bagged 115!

"Pity we can't stick pigs here," lamented one sport, referring to the lancing of wild pigs from horseback.

Bangalore was little better than Ooty. So on November 30, 1896, Amy, now almost twenty-nine, left Bangalore for Tinnevelly. She left the highlands, too. She traveled by train first to Madras, then south to the port of Trichendur, then nearly forty miles up the muddy Tambaravarni River to Tinnevelly. This low country would be much hotter and much more humid than Bangalore—more like Madras. It seemed a plain of silver with all its rice paddies. Palms stuck up here and there and were an important source of matting and the food starch *sago*. Tinnevelly was not as remote as Amy had imagined. The rail service went even beyond the town, farther into the interior. Tinnevelly and Palamcottah, its neighbor across the river, probably totaled fifty thousand natives. Myriad tiny villages added many thousands more.

Hindus outnumbered Muslims ten to one in southern India, so generally the missionaries encountered Hindus. Tinnevelly was very old with a long history—one thousand years at least—of strife between Hindus and Christians. The town not only had a very Anglican church, but a Catholic church with a bishop. Thomas Walker had been there eleven years. As administrator of the Tinnevelly district, he was in the midst of a very agonizing job of purging the church rolls. This was not his idea but that of the missionary society. But as long as he was forced to do it, he insisted on doing it righteously. The missionary society was not happy that he had removed the names of converts who were still living as Hindus. Just as Amy got to Tinnevelly, Thomas Walker did what everyone back in Bangalore had been gossiping about.

"I've resigned from the Church Mission Society," he told Amy as she arrived.

"But I've never belonged to it," she said. "I'm a Keswick missionary."

"Then we had best get on with your study of Tamil."

Thomas started her on not only basic grammar and vocabulary but Tamil classics. "Isn't this a waste of time," she asked, "when I could be studying the Gospel and learning how to preach to them?"

"One must learn first to think like them."

"I'll do it then—against all logic!"

Once he softened and read to her from his own diary. Oh, how he had agonized over Tamil. Yes, with a great deal of effort one could read Tamil, even write it. Then eventually one's ear became tuned and one could understand it when spoken. But to speak it so that the natives could understand it was so difficult. Tamil was a rich language,

96

almost without equal. There was a special word for every shade of meaning. And besides the enormous vocabulary to master, there was an equally enormous reservoir of idioms to learn.

"You set yourself too high a standard," said Amy.

"Oh, you know nothing whatever about it!" snapped Thomas testily.

But Amy forgave him. She had learned that he was under enormous pressure. His independence was much resented by other missionaries. In fact, she soon saw him come out of his study, white as a ghost, yet his eyes burning. He had just read a petition mounted against him—based on lies and jealousy—addressed to none other than the head of the Church of England, the Archbishop of Canterbury!

So was it any wonder Thomas was occasionally cranky? He was by no means humorless. Once he wrote Amy a poem of which one stanza said:

> Who plays the part of kinsman stern,
> And makes my soul with anger burn?
> It is that cold and taciturn
> Annachie.[1]

Annachie was Tamil for "big brother." Yes, Walker was her bossy big brother. And Amy was the pesky little sister who would fight back!

Amy lived with the Walkers in a bungalow. Bungalows of a standard type had been built by the thousands all over India by the British, so the word *bungalow* had a very specific connotation. And, if one was European, one lived in a bungalow. First of all, the bungalow was within a nice-sized compound with walls and well set back from any dusty road. A verandah ran around the bungalow. The interior rooms were large, high ceilinged, and whitewashed. The plan was U-shaped, with bedrooms in the wings. The main part of the house had the living room facing the front, with the dining room behind. Behind the house were quarters for the servants. Also removed from the house was the kitchen, which generated odors and heat and attracted flies. About the only variation in the design of bungalows from one region of India to another was the type of roof: steep pitched in rainy country, flatter pitched in dry country. Furnishings were standard, too, with much rattan furniture on the verandahs, especially the ubiquitous lounge chairs. Flower beds were rarely cultivated. All decorative plants were in huge pots.

"Even you live in a bungalow and employ servants," Amy once said bluntly to Mr. Walker.

"But I don't sip whiskey soda while a boy pulls a *punkah* over my head!" snapped Walker, referring to the great fans hung vertically from ceilings. He regretted his outburst and added, "The Indians expect us to live in a bungalow and give them jobs. You mustn't vary from the norm too much, Amy, or they will shun you completely."

As Amy continued to venture out, she discovered that Thomas Walker was quite right in crushing her desire to live among the Indians. Many of their customs appalled her. For latrines, the Hindus used nearby fields, gutters, alleys, even the floors of their own huts. The waste festered until an Untouchable carried it off. The injustice to Untouchables was staggering. These pariahs—one of every four Hindus—survived by being the sole caretakers of all waste and all death. The sole exception was the waste of the sacred cows. This the devout eagerly gathered.

Walker's resignation freed him and his wife to move. Pannaivilai was also on the Tambaravarni River, closer to the coast, but more in need of the Gospel than Tinnevelly. The town was already pastored by the Reverend Isaac Abraham, a Christian native, but he needed help. The Walkers would rent a bungalow there.

"You may as well come, too," Thomas Walker teased Amy. "I can't very well leave you here so ignorant and only half conversant in Tamil."

In July 1897, the Walkers and Amy moved into a bungalow in Pannaivilai. Amy, who was always independent, began forming a "women's evangelical band." By 1898, at the age of thirty, she had gathered three very devout sisters. Leyal was the pastor's daughter; Sellamuthel, or Pearl, was a young woman with one arm; Ponnammal was a young widowed mother, the daughter-in-law of a convert.

"And they did not ask to be paid," Amy informed the Walkers and told them of the prejudiced perspective in Bangalore that said that a native would help in ministry only if paid to do so.

Amy had adopted the native dress of the Hindus. The Hindu women wore one very long rectangle of coarse cotton cloth, a *sari*. The sari was wrapped securely around the waist twice, then brought up across the chest and over the left shoulder. The remainder hung down the back or was brought up to cover the head. The cotton cloth for the sari usually had one decorated border. Amy's sari was plain white at first. She did not oil her hair as the Indian women did. She tried it once, but the smell offended her. And she wore her bun higher on the back of her head than the Indian women did. In camp, she did not yet cover her head with the sari.

"A sun helmet with a sari?" queried Thomas Walker, referring to the British topee that Amy wore.

The few wealthy Indians wore silks and brocaded clothes, and the poor Indians dressed in simple cotton cloth; but the two main religious cultures could easily be distinguished. The Hindus' garments were "draped"; the Muslims wore "tailored" clothing. In contrast to the sari of Hindu women, the Muslim women wore tailored cotton tops called *choli* and bottoms that were loosely fitted but gathered tight at the ankles. They often added a cloth to cover the head, as well as to give the clothing a more draped appearance. And, of course, the face was covered by a veil.

Muslim men also wore tailored clothing, while Hindu men had a draped appearance. The Hindu man wore a *dhoti,* a rectangle of cotton cloth wrapped around the waist and securely tucked. He was often uncovered above the waist. Both Hindu and Muslim men usually wore turbans. All Indians wore sandals. Most wore a great deal of jewelry on their fingers, toes, noses, necks, wrists, and ankles. Wealthy men and women of southern India dripped jewelry of gold and precious stones, including lockets hanging from a heavy chain around their necks and an even heavier girdle around the waist. The women added much more adornment, featuring a lavish ornament on the forehead and a lesser bauble in the side of the nose. If they were married, the jewelry was to show how well the husband provided for them. If not, the jewelry was to show what a splendid dowry their father would provide. Even poor women were expected to be adorned with a minimum of two good-sized earrings, ten finger rings, ten toe rings, two necklaces, a dozen wrist bangles, and a dozen anklets—if not gold, silver; if not silver, good brass; if not brass, copper or steel; if not copper or steel, glass.

"Nothing is so shameful as no jewelry at all," confided one Hindu to Amy.

Amy tried to learn as many of the customs of the Hindus and Muslims as she could. Of the Hindu rites, it seemed that three were observed by all castes. Twelve days after birth, a Hindu baby was placed in a swinging cot above twelve candles, and the priest announced the baby's name. A second rite was marriage. The first marriage for a man was almost always arranged. But if he later became wealthy, he could add wives of his own choice—as many as he could afford. Of course, no woman could have two husbands! The third rite was at death. The Hindus believed the soul, trapped in the skull, could be released only by sacred fire. So they burned their dead, making sure the skull was burned up or broken open. Three days later, they scattered the ashes into a river.

Amy was surprised at how many rites the Muslims had taken from the Jews. It seemed the only things the Muslims couldn't eat were blood and pork. Muslim boys also were circumcised, although not before the age of seven. Seven days after birth, a baby was named in a ceremony called *aqiqah*. A Muslim man could have as many as four wives if he treated them as equals. For the dead, a service was given before burial. In the grave, the face of the corpse faced their holy city of Mecca. Two main sects of Muslims had evolved: Sunnites and Shiites. The Sunnites were more pious, more accommodating. The Shiites were mystics yet often quite violent.

"Praise God that India has Sunnites," reflected Amy.

Of course, Amy tried to comprehend their religious beliefs. The Muslims' faith she found rather Jewish but stripped of all the wonder, all the miraculous. It seemed a bare-boned desert religion. Hinduism she found too encompassing, too tolerant. The Hindus were all too ready to embrace Christ, but only to set Him beside their other one thousand gods. Their tolerances seemed as abominable as their intolerances. She knew some of their horrible practices, like burning widows and sacrificing baby girls, had been banned by the British. But she had heard rumors of some current temple practices that she prayed were not true.

"Who can doubt the righteousness of converting such heathens?" she wondered.

Amy and her band were energetic. The locals already called Amy the Musal. *Musal* was Tamil for "rabbit." Amy was always moving, always busy. The natives called the entire band the "Starry Cluster." Amy and her band were admired. The natives honored people who adhered to religious vows. In the one hundred-degree days of hot weather, the Starry Cluster evangelized around Pannaivilai. When the weather was cooler—except for June and October, when the monsoons brought the rain in buckets—they hired a driver to haul them farther afield in a wagon pulled by oxen. It was commonly called a bullock cart and was covered by folded-over mats. The women would camp in clearings, usually by a river, and venture forth from there to the surrounding villages.

> *The swift prayer for an open door; the entrance, all of us watching eagerly for a sign of welcome anywhere—for this was pioneer work, not work in prepared ground, and in scores of the places to which we went no white woman had ever been before. . .[we would] walk until we saw a friendly face—and we almost*

always found one. We usually separated then, and
went two and two, and won our way past the men
who would be sauntering in the front courtyard, and
so penetrated to the women's rooms, or if that proved
impossible, we held an open-air meeting somewhere;
or sat down wherever we could, and waited till
someone came to talk, for we found—at festivals, for
example—that if we sat guru-fashion, on a deserted
verandah, or under a tree, that one by one people
discovered us, and came and squatted down beside us
and asked questions. . . .[2]

It was not unpleasant to wait for the curious. Strains of Indian music teased Amy's ears. Sometimes it was classical music, called in southern India *karnatak,* which was considered less contaminated by Muslim influences than northern music. Typically it was performed by a drummer delivering the rhythm, a guitarist droning with a four-stringed *tanpura,* and for the melody either the peculiar stringed instrument called the *vina,* or the Western violin, or the flute. Often a vocalist joined the three instrumentalists. Amy never felt more in India than when she bathed in their exotic music.

Camp life was congenial, too, if one watched out for scorpions and cobras and one kind of white ant that bit viciously. The women slept on cots with mosquito netting inside a large square tent, twelve feet to a side. The driver and cook slept in a smaller tent. If Thomas Walker was along, he slept in a tiny pup tent. The tent life for evangelism had been pioneered long before by Ragland. Camping itself had been refined and perfected by the British in their many foreign conquests. Very sophisticated and portable equipment was available. The larger equipment all folded up, even bathtubs. Airtight boxes protected valuables. Every utensil was protected by a special cover. Within a short time at a campsite, all gear was unfolded and set up. Experienced helpers could have dinner on the table—with tablecloth and all—in very short order. This art of civilized camping was so old with the British that Amy thought very little about it.

Amy tried to be fair by paying the Starry Cluster when they first ventured forth from Pannaivilai. The sisters refused the stipend. And once in Pannaivilai they astonished Amy.

"Your jewelry is gone!"

They had removed all their jewelry. Amy would never have asked them to surrender their jewelry. The sacrifice seemed beyond belief. What holy women He had selected for Amy's work! And what was the reaction of the Hindus? The fathers who had bought the finery were furious, but many other Hindus respected the women even more because the Hindus honored holiness. The word soon spread to thieves that the Starry Cluster women possessed nothing. It really seemed like the hand of God to Amy.

"Refuge! Refuge!" cried a girl's voice outside the bungalow in Pannaivilai one morning in early 1898.

A girl of sixteen, never seen before by the Walkers or Amy, was calling at the gate. She had gone to a mission school in nearby Perungulam and by reading the Bible had become a believer. In India, in contrast to Japan, one could not be a believer and remain at home. Nevertheless, her relatives besieged the bungalow, demanding that the girl be returned. The Walkers and Amy refused to give her up. They offered her sanctuary. Next, Thomas Walker went about securing legal sanctuary for the girl by seeing the proper authorities.

It was Amy's first real exposure to politics in the state areas that were not ruled by maharajahs. These areas were divided into 250 districts. In each district, the chief administrator was called the collector, a holdover, she supposed, from collecting taxes. The collector was all-powerful. Second in command was the superintendent of police. If a British army regiment was stationed in the district, the regimental commander vied with the superintendent of police for power. But the highest authority within a district was always the collector.

Fortunately, the young refugee was of age, so her independence was entirely legal. Krishna Pillai, a Christian and a poet, dubbed the girl "Jewel of Victory." There was nothing Jewel of Victory's relatives could do legally to get her back. But there were illegal means. Kidnapping was common. But in this case, the relatives chose to punish the perpetrators.

"They've burned the mission school in Perungulam," Mr. Walker told Amy one morning.

Another girl sought sanctuary that same year. Again the Walkers and Amy withstood the storm of protest from relatives. Fortunately she, too, was of age. Krishna Pillai dubbed this girl "Jewel of Life."

Each summer, the Walkers went to Ooty in the highlands. There they stayed with Mrs. Hopwood at her great house called "Farley." She ran it as a haven for missionaries. Amy did not want to go, but the Walkers explained that by escaping the blistering plains in the summer, a missionary could put off much longer a furlough to England. So in the summer of 1898, Amy went to Ooty with the Walkers but brought her two recent refugees with her. Mrs. Hopwood, who was wealthy but devoid of any notions of British superiority, accepted the young girls wholeheartedly. Mrs.

Hopwood and her daughter were much like Amy: blurs of constant activity. But Ooty never seemed so refreshing as when Amy thundered across the greens on a pony. Her hair was flying. No head covering could survive such a charge.

"Irish," explained Thomas Walker sheepishly to the other missionaries in retreat.

After a few weeks of recuperation on soft feather beds, and English breakfasts of bacon, eggs, toast, and marmalade, they returned to the sizzling plains. By early 1899, several converts, including men and boys, were baptized in Perungulam. Most of the girls were sent on to a Church of England Zenana school for converts in Palamcottah. The twenty-mile distance seemed a sufficient barrier to retaliation by relatives.

Amy, compelled to write, had recorded all these events in a manuscript. By late 1898, she had sent it off to a mission society that seemed interested. They quickly returned it. It was far too pessimistic, they said. Couldn't she eliminate the failures and accentuate the successes? They obviously did not know Amy Carmichael. Bosh! She put the manuscript aside.

Then came a real test.

"You are how old?" Amy asked a young girl who had come for sanctuary. The girl was radiant in a crimson and orange sari. Bangles reflected light off her like facets of a diamond. Her eyes were large and warm.

"Eleven," replied the child.

"We cannot keep you here, but you can come here for instruction, if you like."

The girl, named Arulai, did come for instruction. Amy soon learned that her father had enormous pressure on him to stop her from coming. But he was a tolerant man. When the girl became ill and Amy visited the house to nurse her, the father became even more tolerant. His tolerance was impressive in view of the fact that Arulai's cousin was tied up in an attic and tortured for trying to do the same thing Arulai had done.

Once, at the bungalow, Amy heard Arulai praying, "Don't let me go back to the dark, please, Lord! Oh, let me live in the light!"

Amy prayed very hard, too.

But one day the father came to the bungalow. He seemed dejected. He said Arulai could no longer come to the bungalow. Was Arulai to be plunged back into darkness?

No!

When her father reached to take her, his arm fell lifelessly at his side. This phenomenon happened several times.

"What is this?" he finally exclaimed. "It is as if my arm is paralyzed."

"It is the one Lord God of heaven," Amy told him. "He has marked this child as His."

Miraculously, the father relented. Arulai begged to have her younger sister, Mimosa, brought to Christ, too, but the father would not even bring her to the bungalow. Still, Arulai was allowed to remain and live with Amy.

NINE

For five years, Amy had been receiving letters from Robert Wilson. They tore at her heart because he pleaded with her to return. But her return to England was more impossible now than ever before. Now she had in her trust not only the Starry Cluster but Arulai. Arulai's going back into her Hindu family was unthinkable.

So Amy prayed again and again, "Oh, please, God, ease Robert Wilson's heart." And on July 4, 1900, she received a letter from the D.O.M.:

> The Master's Word was brought to me this morning early: "He that loveth son or daughter more than me is not worthy of me." "Bind the sacrifice with cords, even unto the horns of the altar." No drawing back. Amen. May it be so in the strength He gives. It is well to have some gift of value to present to Him Who gave His all for our redemption. Praise Him. . . .[1]

Yes, praise Him for easing Robert Wilson's anguish. And Amy's. What she wanted most of all from England now were books, preferably about other missionaries. She had already read about the giants: Livingstone of Africa, Carey of India, and Hudson Taylor of China. She asked well-wishers to send her books about Coillard of Zambesi or Gilmore of Mongolia. They were a "dose of mental and spiritual quinine."[2]

Thomas Walker was asked to help at a seminary for boys in Dohnavur, a village in the lowlands remote from the railroad and main roads. So the Walkers moved there. And so did Amy and her Starry Cluster, as well as Arulai. Dohnavur —"woe-raw-poor" went its rhyme—had grown up around a Christian church built there in 1824. It was a small enclave of Christian natives, mostly of the palm-climbing caste. From Dohnavur Amy and her Starry Cluster could evangelize thousands scattered in many tiny villages, most within a two-hour walk!

About this time—late 1900—Amy was visited again by Ella Crossley of Manchester. This time Mary Hatch was with her. The two visitors traveled on the evangelistic sojourns with Amy and the Starry Cluster. Ella put her hobby of photography to good use. During their stay the two visitors harangued Amy about her idle manuscript. No, she did not need to embellish it, they assured her, just update it. "We will take it back to England, and with Ella's photographs we will find a publisher!"

Meanwhile, the entire world of missionaries was stunned by news from China. China had been seething with resentment against foreigners ever since the Japanese thrashed them in the Sino-Japanese war, which ended in 1895. The resentment spawned a secret society of Chinese known to Westerners as "Boxers." They were little more than thugs. The dowager empress Tz'u-hsi officially denounced them but knew the Boxers might defuse a lot of bitterness against her own incompetence. In 1900, the empress let the Boxers loose. The rampage was called the Boxer Rebellion. The easiest targets were missionaries, both Protestants and Catholics. By the hundreds they were rounded up, then slaughtered. Hudson Taylor's venerable China Inland Mission lost half its missionaries. In the province of Shansi alone, the CIM lost more than one hundred, including children. *"Sha! Sha! Sha!"* chanted the Boxers. "Kill! Kill! Kill!"

"What of Geraldine Guinness?" cried Amy, remembering her dear friend at the China Inland Mission quarters in London back in 1892.

"Do you mean Mrs. Howard Taylor?" corrected Mary Hatch. "None of the Taylors or the Guinnesses were murdered in the rebellion."

Amy was saddened to learn that William Cooper, who had given her wise counsel in Shanghai in 1894, was murdered in the uprising. Naturally the missionaries in India speculated whether such a thing could happen there. Most concluded that although there was resentment against the British presence, it was not enough to confront British weapons.

"But if our soldiers ever leave, it might be quite a different matter," offered Thomas Walker.

"Leave India?" gasped Amy. Even she felt the British would never leave their crown jewel.

Thomas repeated a bitter joke he had heard. "One Indian asked another, 'Which do you hate more: the British or one of our own moneylenders?' The other Indian answered, 'I hate the British more. The moneylender at least hopes I won't die before I pay him back. The British don't care whether I die or not.'"

But were the Indians such innocents?

Early in 1901 at Dohnavur, five boys from the Pannaivilai area were baptized. One was Supu, one of Arulai's many cousins. Within one week all five boys became deathly sick. Two of the boys died, including Supu. The fact that the malady struck only the five converts seemed a case of poisoning. But in India, where cholera was so common and acted so rapidly, with death in a few hours, one could never be sure. And so Amy could only grieve for the boys.

Cholera was not the only widespread disease. The natives suffered also from malaria, leprosy, tuberculosis, and various parasitic worms. Hookworm was the most common parasite, producing severe fatigue. The most hideous manifestation of a parasite was elephantiasis, gross swellings of certain body parts. Good hygiene offered some protection against diseases, especially cholera. But in the back of Amy's mind grew the need to offer Indians modern medical treatments. What a boon that would be. All the diseases could be treated to some degree. Even the dread leprosy was treatable with chaulmoogra oil. But how would a tiny insignificant mission like Dohnavur ever attract a doctor? In the meantime, the missionaries had to treat the human soul.

In March 1901, Amy and the Walkers visited Pannaivilai after nearly a year's absence. One morning a village woman, a Christian convert, appeared with a small girl in tow. Amy was sitting down drinking tea. The girl gawked so rudely that Amy knew she knew nothing at all about white-faced foreigners with frizzy brown hair. But why was the girl there?

"Preena came to me last night—out of sheer desperation," explained the convert. "She is only seven. She escaped the Hindu temple in Perungulam. Preena is to be a *devadasis*, a 'woman of the temple.' First they teach her to sing and dance for the temple gods. But eventually she will entertain Hindu men who patronize the temple."

A temple prostitute. What an abomination!

"Come up here with me," said Amy in Tamil and lifted the girl onto her lap. "Why, your tiny hands are scarred!"

"From burns," said the convert. "She has been punished for an earlier escape."

"What a brave little soul you have, Preena." Amy hugged and kissed her. The girl melted.

"How desperately she wants that affection from her own mother," said the convert. "But the first time Preena escaped from the temple and ran to her mother—her amma—she was pushed away, right into the arms of her pursuers."

"Amma, I want to stay with you always," sobbed Preena.

Amma! Amy had become the girl's amma, her mother, her protector. "Patience, dear," soothed Amy.

Amy knew how cautious Thomas Walker was. He might want to do a hundred things to placate the Hindus. Besides, this girl was not of age. No district collector would support Amy's sanctuary for her. But when the pursuers arrived—the older *devadasis* women of the temple—and a crowd gathered, it was Preena who suddenly stepped forward.

"I won't go with them!"[3] she screamed.

Miraculously the crowd dissipated. Amy had made an important discovery: The Hindus were so anxious to conceal their evil, they might not appeal to authorities. When Amy and the Walkers returned to Dohnavur, Preena—the

"Temple Child"—went with them. Before they left Pannaivilai, however, Arulai was baptized with Arul Dasan, her cousin who had once been bound in the attic. He, too, went to Dohnavur.

Back in Dohnavur, Amy was startled at the affection she and Preena had for each other. Preena was too young to go out evangelizing with the Starry Cluster, and each time Amy returned to Dohnavur, the child glowed with happiness. Preena was a foreshadowing of a greater calling. Amy was to become "Mother" to forsaken children. "Amma, Amma!" seemed a cry of destiny.

March 7, 1901, marked a great event in Amy's ministry. Preena told Amy and the Walkers about evils they had never suspected. Was there any abomination in India worse than using young girls as temple prostitutes? Once, widows had been burned with their deceased husbands, a vile custom called *sati*. But thanks to protests by missionaries like William Carey, the British had stopped that evil. Once, girl babies were sacrificed to the gods, in reality abandoned to be eaten by wolves or crocodiles. But that horrendous evil had also been stopped by the British, thanks to proof offered by Carey. So in her heart Amy knew using girls for temple prostitutes was about the most evil custom remaining in India. It must be exposed and abolished. Until then she would save as many girls as possible. She would offer sanctuary to "temple girls" and to those likely to become temple girls.

Shortly after Amy's two friends returned to England, they had placed her manuscript with a publisher. The book's pointed title was *Things As They Are*. One passage vividly portrayed one of the more blatant Hindu priests:

*Talk of beasts in human shape! It is slandering good
animals to compare bad men to beasts. . .he is a temple
saint—earthly, sensual, devilish. Now put beside him
a little girl—your own little girl—and leave her
there—yes, leave her there in his hand. . . .*[4]

So there! Publication would be in 1903.

This traffic in temple girls—though true—was well hidden. It was so secretive that many missionaries believed temple prostitution was not true. "Oh, it's just an old scare story!" Even Walker felt that way. But he was alarmed enough by Preena to seek information from the seamier elements of Hindu life. Slowly over the next several years he convinced himself of the truth. Girls were indeed sold to the temples, and it was worse than that. Infant boys were bought by temples, too, to be used to satisfy temple patrons or to be resold later to itinerant acting troupes. Was there no form of perversion not offered by temple priests?

"But how well they hide these vile practices from the authorities," worried Amy. "Even Walker had not known."

Once Amy and her Starry Cluster were far south of Dohnavur, sleeping in a stable. Through the walls they overheard a transaction. A priest was negotiating with a father for his daughter. Amy sought help from a missionary doctor in Neyyoor, Howard Somervell. Somervell had the courage of a lion. They rescued the girl. But rescuing children already being defiled in temples seemed virtually impossible. They were so well guarded. Yet orphan girls began to come to Amy. By June 1901, Preena—nicknamed Elf—had been joined by four scamps nicknamed Imp, Pickles, Brownie, and Tangles. They all called Amy "Amma."

The rest of Amy's retinue was growing, too. She had five convert girls. The Starry Cluster had grown by two more. Marial was a small sturdy woman, very independent. Another was "Blessing," who had a habit that drove Amy wild. As Blessing talked, she would shake her hair down, then twist it up on her head again. She was very slow and deliberate.

"Are you an elephant to walk so slowly?" Amy would blurt at Blessing sometimes in exasperation.

Amy was ever Musal, the rabbit. She never idled. She never even walked. She scurried! As more and more children were brought to Amy, she traveled less and less. She would have to decide if Dohnavur was a good place for an orphanage for it now seemed her calling. She had at last remembered the incident in a Belfast tea shop so many years before. She had sampled dainties with her mother, while outside a small girl, barefoot and hardly clad, shivered in the cold rain! How could Amy have forgotten her promise?

> *When I grow up and money have,*
> *I know what I will do,*
> *I'll build a great big lovely place*
> *For little girls like you.* [5]

At age thirty-three, Amy certainly was grown-up. It was time to build a lovely place, to deliver little girls from a life of shame. The children were such a joy with their innocence, too. "A rock is a baby mountain, isn't it?" chattered one. "Do fish love Jesus, too?" chittered another.

In August 1902, Amy admitted in a letter, "Oh, I am getting so hungry for another child!" [6] Yes, her work with children now seemed paramount. Her itinerant tent life was drawing to a close. "The children will tie you down," some protested. Well, why not? Why could she not be tied down for the sake of her Lord whose feet were once nailed?

Near the old whitewashed Christian church, the Walkers and Amy had found a run-down mud-brick bungalow, approached through an avenue of delicate acacia-like tamarinds. The trees seemed giant ferns with their delicate leaves. Goats nibbled scruffy grass that grew on the rust-colored grounds. A gang of beady-eyed macaque monkeys studied these gentle newcomers. Four tiny cottages were also part of the compound. A few miles southwest was an alpine-spiked peak of the Western Ghats called the Holy Washerwoman.

"This truly seems the opening scene of something wonderful," said Amy.

Ella Crossley and Mary Hatch, her friends from Manchester, visited again in 1903. They traveled with Amy on one of her last such ventures. Once near the temple village of Kalakadu, they stopped to look over a wall at a pond full of beautiful white lotus blossoms. "Let us gather some," suggested someone. "They belong to the temple!" someone in the Starry Cluster shot back. Suddenly Amy had a vision. The smallest—the lotus buds—were lifting their innocent faces to the light. Words from Ezekiel boomed into her mind: *"Behold, all souls are mine"!* Yes, how could she accept the contention that the lotus buds—the innocents—belonged to the temple? They belonged to the Lord. After that, Amy often thought of the temple children as "lotus buds."

In late 1903, Thomas Walker's wife was so ill he had to take her back to England. Amy's friends also returned to England. With the Walkers and her friends gone, she began to brood. On December 16 she turned thirty-six. In her heart she had consecrated herself to saving temple children. But where were they? Was her new calling mere folly? She prayed fervently for lotus buds. On March 1, 1904, a pastor from the northern part of the Tinnevelly district arrived at Dohnavur. He carried a baby girl, a wispy thirteen days old. *Another orphan?* thought Amy. *And so tiny.*

"I saw a group of temple women in the night," said the pastor. "They were ushering several of their small victims to the temple. I prayed, and God commanded me to barge in among them. The Lord delivered this baby to me."

"Then this is a temple baby!" gasped Amy.

"Let me name her! Let me name her!" It was Preena, the first temple child.

"Then do," said Amy.

"Amethyst!"

"From Revelation?"

"Yes. Amethyst is one of the twelve foundations of the Celestial City."

"What an imagination you have!"

The Starry Cluster now numbered seven. Ponnammal was Amy's greatest help with the children. Pearl was nearly her equal. But a new member, Devai, was without equal at ferreting out children in peril. She was an older woman, shuffling but driven. It seemed she was always on the trail of some child. Did she ever sleep? More often than not she failed. But how she persevered. It was Devai who brought most of the new children in. By June 1904 Amy had seventeen children at Dohnavur.

"Six of whom were saved from temple prostitution!" Amy said.

In November 1904, Thomas Walker returned, without his wife, who needed more time in England, but with

Amy's mother! Mrs. Carmichael was just in time. Amy not only needed her motherly comfort but her motherly advice. Caring for the children—especially the babies—was overwhelming. And Amy had neither nurse nor doctor to help her. Indian women—even Christians—refused to wet-nurse. What was she to do with the babies she had? They tried goat milk. They mixed in other ingredients to make their own "formula." Amy worked ceaselessly. Often she was awake half the night hovering over a sick child in the nursery. But several of the babies worsened, including Amethyst, who soon died. So did a second baby! A third baby, Sapphire, or "Indraneela" in Tamil, also became sick. She was older, and her baby antics had endeared her to everyone. Indraneela was often in Mrs. Carmichael's lap. She called her "Ahta" for grandmother. When Indraneela died January 6, 1905, Amy had to console herself with words written long ago by Samuel Rutherford:

> *You have lost a child? Nay, she is not lost to you who is found to Christ; she is not sent away, but only sent before, like unto a star which going out of sight doth not die and vanish, but shineth in another hemisphere; you see her not, yet she doth shine in another country. If her glass was but a short hour, what she wanteth of time that she hath gotten of eternity; and you have to rejoice that you have now some treasure laid up in heaven. . . . There is less of you out of heaven that the child is there. . . .[7]*

After Amy had consoled herself with the fact that Indraneela was with the Lord, she wrote a poem:

Dear little feet, so eager to be walking
      But never walked in any grieving way,
Dear little mouth, so eager to be talking
      But never hurt with words it learned to say,
Dear little hands, outstretched in eager welcome,
      Dear little head that close against me lay—
Father to Thee I give my Indraneela,
      Thou wilt take care of her until That Day.[8]

Amy resolved to keep the sixth day of the month as a day of prayer for imperiled children, for not only had Indraneela gone over to God on that day, but Preena had escaped the temple on the sixth day of March. In unguarded moments Amy was stung by the accusation that the deaths of the babies were the fault of well-intentioned but bungling do-gooders! Surely that was Satan attacking. Amy armored herself with the words of her Lord: "Fear not, little flock; for it is your Father's good pleasure to give you the kingdom." And in her heart she knew God wanted her to continue.

On June 19, 1905, Robert Wilson also went to join the Lord. The abandonment of her D.O.M. weighed heavily on Amy. It was another of those burdens missionaries carry. Few earnest missionaries escaped being accused of neglecting their loved ones. David Livingstone and William Carey were but two that the "world," with its secular sentiments, could not understand—would never understand. At least during her grief over Robert Wilson and the three babies, Amy had the comfort of her mother. Mrs. Carmichael stayed until March 1906, making it a very full fifteen-month stay in India.

By 1906, Amy knew that the tragic deaths of the babies had been caused by a mysterious epidemic. No babies

Amy CARMICHAEL

had died since. Still, the family needed medical help, and they had outgrown their facilities at Dohnavur. Children were being rescued at the rate of one a month. The family totaled more than fifty now. Sometimes Amy laughed as she remembered her naive expectations. Never had she envisioned that instead of evangelizing, her mission would be to trim thousands of tiny toenails and fingernails!

The youngest wore simple pullover dresses—blue, of course. Her older girls all wore saris, usually white. Unlike poor Tamil women who wore nothing underneath the sari, they wore petticoats and a blouse—usually yellow—with sleeves past the elbow. Amy also wore a sari, hers creamy yellow, white, or lavender, with a blouse of coordinating color. And no clothing of Dohnavur was other than opaque.

Their overcrowded nurseries were simple enough, little more than mud-brick walls with thatched roofs and dirt floors. Furnishings were grass-mat beds and plain cupboards for the few belongings. She began earnest prayer for more land and buildings that would house a new nursery or two, a schoolroom, and quarters for the workers. *Fired-brick walls, too, Lord.* And red-tiled floors that busy little hands could chalk. None of that had materialized yet; the purchase of a typewriter had been a major item. So they set about remedying not only overcrowding but lack of professional medical care.

A bungalow became available at Neyyoor to the south, near Somervell's London Missionary Society hospital. So Amy had her most trusted helper, Ponnammal, go there with the most vulnerable children. The family continued to grow. Between Dohnavur and Neyyoor it now numbered seventy.

By Easter of 1907, after six of the children had been

120

baptized, Thomas Walker insisted that Amy depart for Ooty before the hot weather set in.

As she prepared to leave, Thomas Walker gasped, "Why are all these children carrying bundles?"

"They're going with me."

"But you are supposed to rest in Ooty."

"I'm only taking twelve of them!"

At Ooty, Amy bolstered herself with words from *The Spiritual Letters of Pere Didon:* "This sacred work demands not lukewarm, selfish, slack souls, but hearts more finely tempered than steel, wills purer and harder than diamond."[9] So there!

Of course, Amy did not agree with Catholicism in its obedience to a pope and its plethora of sacraments, but she never hesitated to gain inspiration from Catholics who lived in Christ. Why should she not be inspired by Thomas à Kempis and Brother Lawrence and the great Augustine? To accept less was to deny what some worthies had done for Christ.

Meanwhile, she finished writing another manuscript about her own work for the Lord and sent it off to England. It would be titled *Overweights of Joy*. Without being dishonest, she tried to make it more joyous than her first book. Reception to *Things As They Are* had been mixed. Negative criticism claimed she had painted much too dismal a picture; Indian paganism couldn't be that bad. But the book sold well, and in the second printing the publishers added testimonies by experienced missionaries from India affirming that Amy had in fact painted a very real picture.

The year 1907 was a blessed year. Amy learned that a woman—in the same vein as Kate Mitchell of Belfast—

wanted to make a large donation, which would enable them to build. . .more nurseries! Soon bricks were being laid. Ponnammal and all her charges could be brought back from Neyyoor because now Amy also had her first real medical practitioner, Mabel Wade, a nurse from Yorkshire. Amy was thrilled when Mabel exclaimed, "Have I been here only a few hours? I feel like I am really at home."

Occasionally, Dohnavur had a real teacher volunteer for a short stint, but as yet they had no regular teaching staff. But the Indian helpers were growing in number. Several were offspring of those already supporting Dohnavur. Ponnammal's daughter, Purripu, appeared to be as industrious as her mother. Another was Pappammal, granddaughter of Krishna Pallai, the Christian poet in the Pannaivilai area. Volunteering must not have been Pappammal's idea, however, because she slouched in, expecting to be overwhelmed by the gloom.

"Instead," she gasped, "Dohnavur overwhelms me with love and joy!"

In the meantime, they fought for the souls of the children. On March 10, 1909, a woman bedecked in gold jewelry that obviously established her wealth breathlessly entered the compound with Muttammal, her very undersized twelve-year-old daughter. The mother was living in sin, so she could not keep her. The girl's father had died, making her heir to a substantial amount of land. Muttammal's uncle wanted control of her. Her life was in great danger. People in India died so easily; treachery might be suspected but could seldom be proved.

"I've heard of Dohnavur since I was only eight," Muttammal said boldly to Amy. "I want to grow up good. Won't you protect me?"

"I may not be able to," answered Amy honestly. "This may be a legal matter."

"But I've always heard your God answers prayers!"

"Stay here, then," said Amy. "We will pray."

TEN

Weeks of bantering began between Muttammal's uncle and the Christians at Dohnavur. Meanwhile, the uncle coerced the mother to change sides. Now she demanded that the girl live with her uncle. Hooligans hired by the uncle threatened Amy once but did not harm her. Amy, who rarely had a moment to spare, was absorbed with the problem. Her writing was the activity that had to be put aside. Two more of her books had been published: *Beginning of a Story* in 1908 and *Lotus Buds* in 1909.

"But it may be a good long time before I find time to write again," she admitted.

She sought the help of the highest British official in the district, the collector. He expressed his sympathy but insisted that the uncle had every legal right to take custody of the girl. Amy traveled to several towns trying to enlist a powerful lawyer. All shunned the case. The uncle had every right to the girl! Finally she tried a lawyer who had just returned from England. He was both Tamil and Christian. Amy begged him to save the girl.

"Can we pray together?" she asked the surprised lawyer. And they knelt.

Miraculously the lawyer accepted the case and negotiated a settlement. Muttammal could remain at Dohnavur, but she must not break caste or be baptized before she came of age. Amy was delighted, even though not breaking caste meant the girl had to have her own food prepared, a very real inconvenience to Dohnavur. Her denial of baptism was inconvenient, too. Yet there was hope.

"My prayer was answered!" cried Muttammal.

But when Amy told Muttammal she would have to prepare her own food, she sulked. She came from a wealthy background. High-caste girls like her did not cook! So Amy asked Muttammal to tell her what was meant in John 21:12–13: "Jesus saith unto them, Come and dine. And none of the disciples durst ask him, Who art thou? knowing that it was the Lord. Jesus then cometh, and taketh bread, and giveth them, and fish likewise." Muttammal read it over and over.

"I see now," sighed Muttammal. "The Lord cooked the fish. Forgive me, Amma."

Muttammal gloried in Dohnavur. Discipline was hard, but she enjoyed the wonderful games the children enjoyed, as well as adopting one of the pesky macaque monkeys for her own. Tumbie was his name.

Despite the intervention by the Christian lawyer, Muttammal's uncle continued his efforts to gain custody of her. Besides fending off constant legal assaults, Amy had to make sure Muttammal was watched at all times. Finally the uncle found a willing judge. On March 27, 1911, the judge decreed that Amy must not only return Muttammal to the uncle within one week but pay all court costs as well. All previous agreements were void.

Amy went to Mabel Beath, a woman from England who was visiting her missionary sister, Frances, at Dohnavur. "Are you willing to help Muttammal even at the risk of a prison sentence?"

Mabel was stunned. Finally she said, "Yes."

That very night, Muttammal disappeared.

The authorities were furious, especially the superintendent of police. Police and their spies watched Amy and Thomas Walker night and day. Thomas was especially suspect when he had to take his wife to England again. Finally they started watching Mabel Beath, too. After she returned to London, an Indian showed up at her house in a very transparent attempt to find Muttammal. Of course, Muttammal wasn't there. Mabel had merely taken the first step of many in the actual escape plan. Amy had anticipated what great wealth could do in tracking Muttammal. So Mabel had disguised Muttammal as a Muslim boy and spirited her to a waiting wagon. From there Muttammal passed from willing hands to willing hands. Eventually she ended up in Ceylon! But even that was not the end of the escape plan. Amy had approached a missionary named Handley Bird. She scarcely knew him, but she told him everything.

"Won't you help Muttammal take the next steps?"

"But what are they?"

"Pray that God will tell you."

Handley Bird sighed. "Well, then, I'm off to Ceylon."

It would be many years before Amy learned Muttammal's fate. She would always think of Handley Bird as the magnificent "Greatheart" of Bunyan's *The Pilgrim's Progress*. For it was Greatheart who guided the pilgrims on the Way to the Celestial City. Yes, it was Greatheart whom the giant Maul—a servant of Satan—confronted on the Way: "Kidnapper, thou gatherest up women and children, and carriest them into a strange country, to the weakening of my master's kingdom." It was Greatheart who replied, "I am a servant of the God of Heaven. . .I am commanded to do my endeavour to turn men, women and children from Darkness to Light, and from the power of Satan to God. . . ."

"God go with you, Greatheart," Amy prayed.

And how like evil to cast the good as the villain! Hadn't it just happened to her? No charges were pressed against Amy for the disappearance of Muttammal, though not for lack of effort on the uncle's part. There was no evidence. His lawyers advised him he could just as easily be accused of being the kidnapper as Amy. But Amy nevertheless was responsible for court costs, which were sizable. She had no funds for the debt. Would she go to prison on that account? British officials of the district were very angry with her now. Then one day the exact amount of the court costs showed up in the mail in a check from a publisher. The publisher insisted he knew nothing of her legal problems, although he had had an overwhelming compulsion to send her the money!

In 1911, Amy brooded over boys, too. Why were she and her helpers not saving boy babies? They knew boys were also sold to the temples. She put the matter before Thomas Walker. He was troubled, too, but advised her not to take boys unless it was absolutely necessary. Her efforts were spread thin as it was. And mixing boys and girls in a facility as limited in size as theirs was inviting trouble. Unhappily, Amy tried to set aside her desire to save boys.

In August 1912, a five-year-old child named Lulla was dying in the nursery. Her labored breathing, growing worse every second, disturbed Amy so much she could not bear to watch. She went outside into the night and prayed for the Lord to take the child. Her suffering must stop.

"Amy, come into the nursery, quick," whispered Mabel Wade into the darkness.

Amy entered to see the child smiling and holding her arms out to someone no one else could see. The child clapped her hands in glee! Then she passed away. Amy was stunned. She had witnessed a Christian passing into the Lord's glory! That miracle helped Amy cope with the rest of that tragic August.

First, Mrs. Hopwood of Ooty died. Oh, how Amy had enjoyed Mrs. Hopwood pointing out the "Delectable Mountains" and "Beulah Land" in the distant heights, for Mrs. Hopwood, too, loved *The Pilgrim's Progress*. Amy had often thought that Mrs. Hopwood's counterpart in *The Pilgrim's Progress* was "Discretion," of the House Beautiful atop the Hill of Difficulty. For surely Mrs. Hopwood had been a saint to all tired travelers on the Way to Salvation.

But Amy had no such consoling thoughts on August 24, when she read a telegram from the village of Masulipatam. It just wasn't possible! "Thomas Walker is dead!"

Thomas was only about fifty years old when he died. Unfair! What had happened? It was so incredibly swift. Snakebite? Food poisoning? But what did it matter? He was dead. And Amy fought using her own grief as a form of self-pity. Yes, it would be very difficult to continue on in Dohnavur without the wisdom and strength of Thomas

Walker holding her up. And Ponnammal would be heart-broken. She had been so close to Mr. Walker that she had virtually considered him her father. He was Ponnammal's D.O.M. Mrs. Walker was still back in England. She would be the most devastated of all. Amy forced herself to be strong. Even though her own heart was breaking, she would have to comfort these grieving souls, assuring them again and again that Thomas was in the lap of the Lord.

"Well, if I never write anything else again, I will write the story of Thomas Walker of Tinnevelly," sobbed Amy.

She had Mr. Walker as much in mind as herself when she wrote a poem called "The Calm Community of the Criticized" for *Made in the Pans,* a book she was already working on:

> *If, though all unawares, and not of ill intent,*
> *Thou steppest one inch outside the beaten track;*
> *If thou in deed or word or preference*
> *Depart from the Accustomed, or ransack*
> *The unexplored, bright treasure-mines of life*
> *And drawing forth their jewels make the House*
> *Religious, as men call it, a glad place—*
> *O then hide thy face. . . .*[1]

Learning that Thomas Walker had died of food poisoning helped her not at all. She didn't indulge in the hapless "if only he had not done this or if only he had done that" lament. A person of faith could not do that. God was the Master of history.

Over the next few weeks, aided by an exchange of letters with Mrs. Walker, Amy emerged stronger. She was, just as Mrs. Walker wrote, driven closer to God. Every man falls and every woman falls—"as grass: as a flower of the field"—but God is always. And other missionaries of southern India rallied around her. Mr. Carr came from Palamcottah and played the organ every evening. Amy's grief was salved by joyous hymns sung by her little songbirds. Agnes and Edith Naish, two teaching missionaries, arrived almost immediately to take over the teaching for Amy. It was the first time the children really had professional tutors. Arul Dasan arrived to help with the management of Dohnavur. It was no small operation, now nourishing in body and spirit well over one hundred Christians.

The year 1913 held no relief for Amy. Ponnammal became very sick and had to be taken to the Salvation Army Hospital in the large city of Nagercoil near Neyyoor. The diagnosis was a virtual death sentence: cancer. There was a chance the cancer might be surgically removed. So Ponnammal endured surgery, then after that attempt had to suffer it a second time. Meanwhile, Amy got the shocking news that on July 14 her mother had died. Her mother had traveled to Canada to visit Amy's brother Alfred and had only recently written encouragement to Amy that Ponnammal would recover in "God's mighty protecting Arms of love and care."[2]

"How is it possible?" grieved Amy. She forced herself to recite her mother's favorite verse, "The LORD is good, a strong hold in the day of trouble."

Mother had comforted Amy with it when her father died in 1885. Amy could also take comfort in what her mother had done. After all, mother was nearly seventy, the Bible's allotted "threescore years and ten." Mrs. Carmichael had been far more to Amy than simply a loving mother. She had served Amy as her main representative in England, which entailed some publicizing of the good work in Dohn-avur. Otherwise, how could Amy have received one day in 1912 a letter of encouragement from the queen? Yes, Queen Mary, wife of King George VI, wrote Amy. Thanks to her books and her mother, Amy was no obscure missionary.

By October, Mrs. Irene Streeter, wife of Canon Streeter of Oxford, became Amy's main representative in England. Mrs. Streeter had visited Dohnavur twice. "Except for my mother," said Amy, "Mrs. Streeter is the dearest friend in England that our work could ever have."

Poems of comfort often just came to Amy. She could be suffering a midnight headache or bumping along in a stuffy bullock cart. Once she scribbled a poem on the brown wrapper of a medicine bottle she was bringing from Nagercoil:

> I have no word,
>   But neither hath the bird,
> And it is heard;
>   My heart is singing, singing all day long,
> In quiet joy to Thee Who art my song.
>   For as Thy majesty
> So is Thy mercy,
>   So is Thy mercy.
> My Lord and my God.[3]

Life rushed on for Amy. The next episode in her life involved the beautiful curly-headed child called Kohila. Kohila arrived at Dohnavur in December 1913. Her first day became her "Coming Day." This day would be celebrated every year like a birthday. An arrival's actual birthday was rarely known. On the Sunday preceding the Coming Day, the child's room was festooned with flowers. She was given a special card with a small gift like scented soap. At the evening hymn singing, the child was garlanded with flowers.

But Kohila's peace was short-lived. Like Muttammal's relatives, her family members threatened to bring a lawsuit against Amy if the child was not returned. And once again Amy had to find her Greatheart. This time it was Arul Dasan who spirited the child away. For weeks, Amy wondered whether she would be arrested for her defiance. When Arul returned, she was even more apprehensive. But nothing happened. Was Amy tolerated by British officials now like some incorrigible pest too clever to catch and too popular to harass?

In August 1914, all attention was diverted by the beginning of a colossal war in Europe. Some British missionaries said the war began as a local skirmish between Austria-Hungary and Serbia. But convoluted alliances mushroomed the skirmish first into a European war, then into a world war, the first in mankind's bloody history.

"At least Britain did not start this abomination," said one missionary with little satisfaction.

"Will war come to India?" asked many of the children.

"No," answered Amy, "there are no colonies of the warring factions adjacent to each other."

But that was not true of Africa. War raged between Britain's Nigeria and Germany's Cameroon. And Amy did not bother to tell the children that it was likely that Indian soldiers would be sent to the war. In fact, both Hindus and Muslims rallied to the British cause. The native drive toward nationalism had been dormant, especially since, as the British had hoped, the Muslims had founded the Muslim League and thus fragmented the native effort. If the Indian National Congress and the Muslim League ever united, who knew what might happen to the British in India?

"There's a Hindu lawyer up in Bombay who might emerge as the real leader of India someday," said one missionary in Madras. "I heard him speak here not long ago. He made quite an impact in South Africa—especially advancing the lot of the Tamil-speaking Indians working there. He's pushing *swaraji,* or 'India for the Indians.' He was educated in London, yet wears nothing but a *dhoti.* He endorses a simple native diet and cottage industries. He is honest. Many Indians already regard him as holy."

"Holy?" said a startled Amy. "Who is he?"

"Mohandas Gandhi."

Amy had her own struggles. Ponnammal was dying of cancer and was in agony. The wasting away of Amy's dear friend was doubly painful because of Ponnammal's constant regret that she was deserting Amy. "You must bear the burden alone," lamented Ponnammal. Once when she seemed in unendurable pain, she told Amy, "If the pain does not get any greater than this, I can stay and help you." Such devotion ripped at Amy's heart. Finally the pain was so bad, Ponnammal was virtually comatose from doses of morphine. Yet she lingered on. She had suffered for over two years. The shadow of the valley of death took on new meaning for Amy. It was so much longer, so much denser, a thousand times more dreadful than she had known. *Why, God, why? But Your will be done.* On August 26, 1915, the Lord took Ponnammal.

"Praise God for His mercy."

It had been eighteen years since Ponnammal joined Amy's Starry Cluster. What a great foundation she had been. The first and the brightest. Pure gold. Amy had to wonder at herself. She was forty-seven years old now, and any thoughts of marriage—other than to Christ—were long gone. Moreover, she was "Amma," the mother of dozens of girls and boys.

Arulai returned from Ooty with Bright's disease, or nephritis. The sweet child had already survived typhoid and a mild attack of tuberculosis. Now this. By December Arulai was "at the Gates." She heard celestial music just as Ponnammal had. She even saw Thomas Walker and Ponnammal waiting to greet her. Amy wired friends of Arulai that she was dying.

"Must You take her too, Lord?" Amy cried out angrily. "First Walker, then my mother, then Ponnammal, now Arulai. Why? Why? Why?"

A friend from Palamcottah rumbled his wagon over the rough roads all night to reach Dohnavur. His only wish was to see the love in Arulai's warm brown eyes just one more time. He feared he would only see her buried. But on the morning of December 7, he witnessed a miracle. Arulai had improved.

"Recovery is so rare in the tropics," reflected Amy. "And death is so common."

It was such a blessing when things turned out well. Another blessing soon followed. Kohila appeared, hoping that, after many months of exile, she had been forgotten by her relatives. Would Muttammal return someday also? Arulai had long prayed that not only would Muttammal return one day but marry her cousin Arul Dasan! Amazingly, Amy later dreamed the same thing, specifically that Muttammal and Arul Dasan would marry in a church in Ceylon. By this time, Amy knew that Handley Bird had taken Muttammal to China. Back in 1911, her "Greatheart" had gone all the way to Nanning in the province of

Kwangsi. There he left Muttammal with Dr. Lechmere Clift and his wife. So Muttammal had been safe with a good Christian family all those years.

Now in 1915 Arulai and Amy talked to Arul Dasan. He agreed to let them arrange a marriage!

"We'll write at once," said Amy.

Who knew how Muttammal might feel about it? Or the Clifts? But Amy soon knew her dream had come from above. Muttammal and the Clifts were in complete agreement. But when and how? Letters flew back and forth.

By 1916 Amy had received her finished life of Thomas Walker, titled simply *Walker of Tinnevelly*. The story seemed almost petty, the cover blurb by Eugene Stock gratuitous, when hundreds of thousands of soldiers were being slaughtered in the soggy trenches of Europe. And Walker would not have approved of a book about himself at all. Yes, destroy the self. Realize one's own littleness. God's mightiness. Amy felt enormous shame on seeing the finished book. Had she done no more than glorify herself?

"I need spiritual partners," she admitted.

Eleanor McDougall, principal of the Women's Christian College in Madras, became one such partner. When Amy first met her, she visualized Eleanor as the embodiment of a Tamil proverb: "Better to plow deep than plow wide." Eleanor plowed deep. She knew many of the mystical writers Amy knew. Together they spent many hours in prayer and discussion of the great mystics. But Eleanor, spiritually helpful as she was, could visit Amy only occasionally. So on March 18, 1916, Amy started a group of spiritual sisters. She was inspired by *The Imitation of Christ,* the small classic of holy life. Thomas à Kempis drew much of his inspiration from the other holy brothers in his own order, a lay group with no vows. The brothers strived to imitate the lives of Christ and the apostles and lived in a community that shared food and shelter. They were not to live apart from the world like monks. They worked as common men during the day, consequently their name: "Brothers of the Common Life."

"Thus today we launch the 'Sisters of the Common Life,'" Amy explained to the seven women she had invited.

The sisters included Arulai and Preena. All, like Amy, had decided they wanted to live in Christ without the distraction of marriage. Every Saturday, they met in a wooded area to discuss God and holiness. Amy indulged this meeting in English. It was justified because that way she could share her favorite writers with the sisters without the exhaustion of trying to translate every word. Only the Bible and *The Pilgrim's Progress* were available in Tamil. Energy would be conserved and spent in God's glory. She shared her favorite passages from Thomas à Kempis, of course, but also other ancient worthies like Brother Lawrence, Richard Rolle, Raymond Lully, and Julian of Norwich. Samuel Rutherford and the inexhaustible John Bunyan were very dear to her, too. Her more modern favorites included the missionaries Josephine Butler of India and Bishop Moule of China.

"The Cross is the attraction,"[4] the sisters constantly reminded themselves. They had a creed of sorts:

My Vow:
Whatsoever Thou sayest unto me, by Thy grace I
will do it.

My Constraint:
Thy love, O Christ, my Lord.

My Confidence:
Thou art able to keep that which I have committed
unto Thee.

My Joy:
To do Thy will, O God.

My Discipline:
That which I would not choose, but which Thy love
appoints.

My Prayer:
Conform my will to thine.

My Motto:
Love to live; live to love.

My Portion:
The Lord is the portion of mine inheritance.[5]

Prayer was essential. And it was deep, practiced prayer. For many years Amy could feel the presence of a distraction in group prayer. Time had not dulled her sensitivity. Was one of the girls thinking about something else? She would stop the prayer and demand that love be restored. Girls! "Thou shalt love the Lord thy God with all thy heart, and with all thy soul, and with all thy mind. This is the first and great commandment."

Service was essential, too. The sisters took on jobs no one else wanted to do. But they did it with joy. Joy was vital. After all, joy was one of the fruits of the Holy Spirit. If it was lacking, it signaled a spiritual lack, perhaps a lack of desire to do the Lord's will. Sometimes when Amy was alone, she reflected on Walker, Ponnammal, and her mother. If she had feelings of sadness, she became very upset with herself.

"I must remind myself to live in the joy of those gone, not grovel in the sense of my loss."

She angrily scribbled that into her diary October 10, 1916. For although the outside world and even those close by Amy perceived her as a busy, busy woman, Amy was constantly seeking holiness. Even so, occasionally she was prey to attacks that no one can prevent.

ELEVEN

Nightmares.

Amy began having dreams that frightened her very much. On January 16, 1917, she wrote in her diary, "O forgive me, but I *must* ask it: take me quickly when my work is finished. Do not, I beseech Thee, let me be disabled by pain or inability and live on as a burden to others. Have been more than usually in pain these last few days."[1]

"Oh, God," she prayed, "don't let this dream be a premonition that I might someday be disabled, even an invalid. Is the devil trying to trick me?"

But Amy's anxieties were usually on behalf of others. Perhaps it was not apparent to those who saw her quick decisions, but, oh, how she lamented the girls who lost their way. "Is the work for these girls going to end in dust and ashes?"[2] she wrote unhappily in her diary. Then she remembered a gift to Dohnavur perhaps not handled properly. "Burn, burn out of me any insincerity that lurks within."[3] The memory of Ponnammal's agony haunted her, too. And Dohnavur now wrestled with emergencies in twelve nurseries!

Discipline on the children was strict. They were not allowed to be slackers. A few were rebellious, reminding Amy of herself as a child. Dohnavur harbored many endearing stories of the antics of children now. Every parent has a hundred stories. Amy had a thousand. She gave every child a good-night kiss and she would continue to do so until there were not enough minutes in the evening to do it. Love was their blanket.

One game the children played was acting out a poem as Amy recited it:

> Our mother was a butterfly,
>   We are her little eggs,
> Inside us caterpillars lie,
>   Young things with many legs.
> I am a little caterpillar,
>   Very soft and fat,
> I'll change into a chrysalis,
>   What do you think of that?
> I am a little chrysalis,
>   And very still I lie;
> For folded up inside me
>   Is a little butterfly.
> I am the little butterfly,
>   I want to fly about;
> I'm so tired of being here,
>   Oh, now I'm out! I'm out!
> O kind wind, come and fan my wings,
>   O sunshine, make them dry,

O flower, I come to you! Away,
*   Away, away I fly.⁴*

Many of the children adopted their own special mon-
key among the band that cavorted around Dohnavur. Also
allowed as pets were squirrels, dogs, and exotic animals like
the loris that Amy's people back in England could only
wonder about. Amy loved animals and birds. In fact, her
weakness for birds was becoming legend. Occasionally in
the open market she would be overcome after seeing "little
living jewels" in tiny rickety cages. On those occasions she
would come back to the compound with as many cages as
she could carry! There the birds settled into larger cages or
aviaries. Of course, she made the pets into metaphors.

"Are you Raggles or are you Taggles?" she would sing
to the children of two pet robins. "Raggles was called Raggles because he was always untidy. His feathers hung about
him like rags. He did not take the trouble to tidy himself,
and so Taggles had to try to tidy him, which he did by
pulling those loose feathers out. But the great difference
between the two is this: Raggles expects to have his food
put into his mouth, and Taggles, though he likes to be fed,
takes the trouble to feed himself. Raggles, you see, likes
everything to be done for him, while Taggles does things
for himself and even tries to help his lazy brother. Also
Raggles doesn't come when he is called, and Taggles gladly
does. I like Taggles's disposition very much. Don't you? Are
you Raggles or Taggles?"⁵

In 1917, Muttammal—now twenty years old—finally
consented to marry Arul Dasan. Dr. Clift was due to go to
France as a medical officer. Mrs. Clift was going to America to wait out the war. But first they would all convene in

Colombo, Ceylon, for a wedding. It was just as Amy had dreamed it, down to the last detail! In May, Arul Dasan and Muttammal returned to Dohnavur. It was a great blessing to Amy. Not only was she joyous over seeing Muttammal, now called Kunmunnie to hide her identity, but she needed Arul's help.

Summer retreats were no longer spent in Ooty. It was not because Mrs. Hopwood had passed on, for her daughter was congenial. No, it was because Thomas Walker had always been part of Ooty, too. And Amy's family was so large now, they overwhelmed the accommodations at Farley. In 1915, after Amy had inquired about nearby highland forests, the forest department let her use an empty bungalow located at Sengelteri, a mere eight miles northwest of Dohnavur. Cool air and a waterfall were most refreshing. What a peaceful kaleidoscope—the children dressed in blues and yellows flickering through green and brown forest glades!

The forest was more real than any forest in Rudyard Kipling's *Jungle Book* stories. Real panthers lurked instead of Bagheera, and genuine tigers, not Shere Khan, were to be feared. The bears were real as well, unlike Baloo. Once, Amy, who by now was almost fifty, exercised her wild Irish humor. When she and three girls spotted Pearl and the rest of the group coming back from the river, they hid behind a tree and growled like bears. Their victims flew into a panic. Led by rail-thin Pearl, they danced about and waved flimsy sticks in defense against the forest phantoms.

"Whatever is the matter?" yelled Amy, stepping out from the tree.

"Bears! Bears!" screamed Pearl and the others.

There was no need to explain the hoax after the small girl with Amy fell to the ground in a fit of giggles. How could the family ever stop going to the forest? It was there her little songbirds sang:

> *The elephant comes with a tramp, tramp, tramp,*
> > *The elephant comes with a tramp, tramp,*
> > *tramp,*
> *Through the forest and over marshy ground*
> > *His great big flat feet pound and pound*
> *With a rumpety-dumpety-crumpety sound.*
> > *See, here's a tangle of maidenhair,*
> *Among the pandanus spikes down there;*
> > *And right through the very middle of it*
> *He's trampled exactly as he saw fit*
> > *With his blundery-wondery-dundery wit.*
> *A fool, do you think? No, he's no fool,*
> > *Look at the track, it leads to a pool,*
> *And on and on to a shady place*
> > *Where he can fan his beautiful face*
> *With a jungelly-tumbelly-scrumbelly grace.*[6]

But soon the facility at Sengelteri grew too small. What were they going to do? The forest was such a delight. In the summer of 1917, Amy and others from Dohnavur began looking around for a forested property they might buy for themselves. Amy prayed their wish was not frivolous. Surely the family needed such a retreat. Eventually an old Hindu Brahmin led them to an area called the "Gray Jungle," which lay on the flank of a mountain, below the great forests of teak and sal. Within a thick growth of evergreen oak and chestnut was a river and a waterfall, and the forest opened into a beautiful glade, as if inviting Amy to build a cottage there. The Gray Jungle could be entered only by climbing up a scary cliff. It was perfect.

"The Brahmin tells me you are interested in buying land," said a Muslim who appeared out of nowhere.

"Yes, I might be interested," said Amy, disguising her amazement.

"I am the owner," he said matter-of-factly. "For one hundred English pounds you can own thirty-seven acres of this paradise."

So much! And yet so little.

"Sisters," said Amy, "let us pray: Lord, if it be Your will, may You send us a sign."

It was as if she had thrown out a fleece. That same night, they returned to Dohnavur. In the mail from a lawyer in Ireland was an inheritance bequeathed to Amy by an old friend. The sum was one hundred pounds!

"The Gray Jungle!" screamed someone.

"And a forest house!" piped another, who then added apologetically, "when we get the funds."

On September 17, 1917, the Gray Jungle became the family's legal property. Building in the highlands was difficult, though. It was hard to get laborers up the cliff. And the caste system drove Amy wild. The men who cut down a tree were allowed to do nothing else, and the men whose caste allowed them to saw the tree into planks were not there that day. Then, when the boards were ready, the carpenters were not there. If it rained, none of the men showed up, and the family had to hurriedly cover all the mud walls with mats to keep them from disintegrating. Much of the work had to be done by the family. They made amateur mistakes, with walls collapsing and roofs leaking. But what a wonderful sanctuary the forest house was when the summer sun blistered the plains below.

Near the forest house, the pool swirled out of the ancient core rock of the mountain. The pool was a special place where every child was taught to swim, just as Amy had been taught as a child in the mill pond. Once, they were blessed when two carpenters—captivated by Christ in their meetings—asked to be baptized in the pool. An ordained friend of Amy's was happy to come to the Gray Jungle and oblige:

> *The Pool looked its very loveliest. A rock runs into the heart of it, and on it we can stand. This rock was colored a sort of dull gold that day because of the way the light caught it. On either side the water was jade green, till it reached the rocks which are gray, splashed and veined with crimson, brown and yellow, and their colors were brokenly reflected in the water. A little waterfall tinkled at the other end. This is a pool of many joyful swimming hours. . . . But never was it so happy a pool as that day when those two men confessed Christ crucified. The toil of the house was nothing then. . . .*[7]

Construction of a forest house in no way slowed the expansion of Dohnavur. In fact it seemed to explode. Amy's conscience had been troubling her for some time—at least eight years—about taking only girls. One day in the forest house, God reminded her to take boys. She was stunned. How was this to come about?

Then in January 1918 another baby—this one more than one-year-old but bundled—was delivered into her arms at the gate of the compound. The baby smiled wearily and held out wanting hands. Amy remembered thinking, *What a brainy little head! If only this baby were a boy.* She handed the precocious infant to Mabel.

"It's a boy!" screamed Mabel from the nursery five minutes later.

And thus began their haven for boys. In 1919, Irene Streeter visited to break the ground on yet another nursery, the third of a new series. And she stayed long enough to break the ground on a fourth. Nurseries now numbered more than twenty! But 1919 marked the beginning of great upheaval in India. After the Great War ended in 1918, the little lawyer from Bombay, Mohandas K. Gandhi, who had supported Britain during the war, wanted justice for the Indians. British authorities brushed him aside like a pesky fly. But Gandhi persisted. To his credit, he advocated peaceful resistance. This pleased the British very much. But something happened that no one in India—not even Gandhi—expected. If Gandhi showed up somewhere to file a protest, as he did for sharecroppers in Champaran, within hours there was a sea of peasants by his side. Thousands upon thousands. Only Gandhi could control their anger. Occasionally even he could not restrain his single-minded followers. Riots ended in bloodshed. But the most savage atrocities were committed by the British against the Indians. None signaled British oppression of the Indians more than what happened at Amritsar on April 13, 1919.

Gandhi was not at the rally of peaceful demonstrators. British troops opened fire on them, killing 379 and wounding another thousand. So the terrible thing growing in India was not the move toward nationalism but the immoral force employed by Britain to stop it.

"I don't want to believe such terrible stories," admitted Amy.

To make things worse, 1919 marked the year Amy had become acceptable to that very British establishment. It would be hard to imagine a greater shock than receiving the news from Lord Pentland, Governor of Madras, that she was now included on the Royal Birthday Honors List. It didn't seem that long ago that the district collector and the superintendent of police would have gladly paid her passage back to England or anywhere else!

Then Amy was informed she was the recipient of the Kaiser-i-Hinds Medal for her services to India. She fired a letter to Lord Pentland:

> *Would it be unpardonably rude to ask to be allowed not to have it? . . . I have done nothing to make it fitting, and cannot understand it at all. It troubles me to have an experience so different from His Who was despised and rejected. . . .*[8]

But friends convinced her it *was* unpardonably rude to refuse it. It might even hinder her efforts in Dohnavur. So she relented. But she refused to go to Madras to accept the medal. She wanted no glory.

One day, Arulai's long-lost sister, Mimosa, turned up at the gate of the compound. With her were three of her four sons, one a baby. Mimosa's husband had not allowed the teenage son, Rajappan, to come. Mimosa wanted to leave her four-year-old and her seven-year-old. Amy welcomed them, stunned by Mimosa's haggard appearance. She was two years younger than Arulai but looked much older. Her story was the most heartbreaking story Amy had ever heard. Poor Mimosa had wanted to come to Dohnavur back in 1899, but her father refused. But in the briefest of interludes when Arulai had counseled her, Mimosa had been smitten by the love of Christ. After Arulai had left,

Mimosa existed among the Hindus like an illiterate Abraham, knowing only that she must love the one true God.

She refused to indulge Hindu customs. And she had been a pariah all these years. Her own brothers treated her with the disrespect normally reserved only for Untouchables. Naturally such a woman, who was not practicing Hinduism and getting poorer every year, could find only a lazy scoundrel for a husband. Her life had been ten thousand times harder than Arulai's. Yet she had her one God — whom she worshipped in a primitive but pure way—and she had her four sons.

Years before, Arulai had heard of her plight and written to her. It was the only letter Mimosa had received in her entire life. A cousin condescended to read it to her. She kept it like it was treasure. At long last she had come to Dohnavur to give her sons a chance. If only she, too, could learn to read, she said, so she could savor God's Word. But she had to go back to her husband to try to save the oldest son, Rajappan. Amy's heart ached that Mimosa had to return to that very hard life. Had there ever been such a poor, ordinary, illiterate girl who was so tenacious for Christ? Amy resolved to someday write the story of Mimosa.

Amy continued to write. Writing was like breathing to her. As if she did not have enough to do, she began to write letters to individuals within the compound, too. Of course, she had always written down day-to-day requirements and fired them off to workers; but now she wanted to do something more spiritual, more loving. A good example was the tender note she sent to a troubled child:

I wonder what your biggest temptation is. Is it to be suddenly angry? That was mine when I was a little

girl. I used to feel something like fire suddenly burn-
ing up in my heart. If you feel like that, ask the Lord
Jesus to pour His cool, kind, gentle love into your
heart instead. Never go on being angry with anyone;
be Jesus' little peacemaker. . . .[9]

She also continued to write for the public. It was very important for many reasons that the story of their ministry be told outside India. By 1918 she had added two more books, including one loving tribute to Ponnammal. Now she was writing about their experiences in the Gray Jungle. Poetry still expressed her thoughts best:

Dim green forest
     Of a thousand secrets,
When you were planted
     Did the angels sing?
Many things I wonder,
     Are they all your secrets,
Won't you ever tell me anything?
Great white waterfall
     Breaking through the forest,
Where do you come from,
     Where do you go?
Had you a beginning,
     Will you go on forever?
For ever and for ever will you flow?

Great black, glistening wall
     Veiled in shining glory,
Piled among the waters
     Rock upon rock,

O to have stood and seen
   Hands at work upon you,
Shivering you and shattering shock upon shock.

Deep, dark, silent pool
   Hollowed in the water's foot,
What do you think of
   All the long day?
Do you hear the thunder
   Of tremendous waters?
   Do you hear the laughter of the spray?[210]

Tranquil thoughts.

But when she first encountered Jambulingam, her life was scarcely tranquil. Jambulingam was a notorious robber. He called himself the Red Wolf. The English newspapers labeled him Robin Hood. Amy rather liked that name herself. Just like Robin Hood, he gave rise to stories that were far-fetched. He robbed from the rich to give to the poor. He leaped across wide streams in a single bound. He was a crack shot. No handcuffs could shackle him. No jail could hold him. Like everyone else, Amy was enchanted with the stories. Amy was not shy about asking God for favors, either. So she prayed that she could meet this "Robin Hood." On October 12, 1921, when Amy was returning from the Gray Jungle, a man stepped out in front of her.

"I am Jambulingam," he said.

"Whatever do you want with me?"

"I felt a compulsion to meet you."

Thus Amy learned firsthand about this Robin Hood. He claimed he had been falsely accused of a crime many years before. He panicked and ran. By not clearing his name right away, he gave his accusers the opportunity to soil his reputation even more. He then made another poor choice and turned to crime. Yes, he gave money to the poor, but only to ease his conscience. He was nothing like a "merry" Robin Hood. He was intensely unhappy. While he was running from the law, his wife had died and left his three children to the cruelties of India. It was when Amy learned of the children that she knew the reason God had forced them together.

"I will take your children in at Dohnavur," she offered. "But I urge you to surrender to the police and get this meaningless life behind you."

He refused to surrender, but he did deliver his children to Dohnavur. Five days later, he was captured and savagely beaten. Could Amy doubt that God had brought them together in the most unlikely of meetings to save his three children? She was allowed to visit him in the prison hospital. He was a broken man. She counseled him in the Lord. She gave him a Bible to study and visited him often. She prayed for his soul. Then she dreamed she went to Jambulingam in prison to ask him if he wished to be baptized. He said yes. So she visited Jambulingam in prison and asked him if he wished to be baptized. And he became a Christian just as she had dreamed it.

One day a sister rushed to her. "Jambulingam has escaped!"

No! Why had she considered him safe? Why had she not prayed for him fervently? Why did she not know he could not resist the temptation to escape? Amy was very worried. Yes, he was popular with the people, even with a lot of the British. But among the British lurked the mentality that slaughtered the innocents at Amritsar. One must never forget that. So she prayed that he would give himself up. Yet, new robberies were attributed to him. Amy was certain the crimes were done by others and conveniently blamed on Jambulingam. Efforts of hers to arrange a secret meeting with the fugitive were unsuccessful for many months. She even saw an official who reported to the collector. The official said if Jambulingam would vow that he had committed no more crimes, the officials would believe him. Jambulingam would not be prosecuted for them. Finally she did secretly meet with Jambulingam. He had given up hope. He had made the British officials look foolish. He didn't believe what the official had told Amy. He would be killed in prison for sure. No, it was too late.

"Just promise me you won't die with blood on your hands," said Amy sadly.

He promised.

Amy tried to put aside her worry. Worrying wasn't Christian. Christ's words were plain enough: "Take therefore no thought for the morrow: for the morrow shall take thought for the things of itself. Sufficient unto the day is the evil thereof." And a wonderful thing happened. Arulai's sister Mimosa was rescued at long last. She had come to live at Dohnavur. And the oldest son, Rajappan, was with her. Mimosa had rescued a niece, too, a neglected toddler. What a life Mimosa had led for Christ!

Yes, today had its own troubles. But Amy's problems were now the problems of prosperity and expansion. For her recent acceptance by the Crown caused donations to flood into Dohnavur. Nurseries were under construction constantly. By 1923, they were building the thirtieth! Whereas once they had virtually no boy babies, there were now dozens. Amy had twenty-seven helpers, of whom thirteen were from Britain and Ireland. Chief among the helpers were Pearl, Arulai, and Mabel Wade. And new living quarters had been built for her helpers. The new quarters offered the one luxury enjoyed by these older individuals: privacy. Each had ample water to bathe, as well as a chamber pot.

Dohnavur now even boasted an automobile, which greatly speeded up trips to Palamcottah and Neyyoor. All this she reported in her newsletter, renamed the *Dohnavur Letter* because *Scraps* suggested to some readers the trivial. Readers also became acquainted with a certain nomenclature in Tamil that had arisen for the Dohnavur family. Older girls were "Sitties." Those older sisters in authority were "Accals." The equivalent "big brothers" were "Annachies."

That year of 1923 also marked the end of the Jambulingam story.

TWELVE

N o!" cried Amy when she heard the news.

On September 20, 1923, Jambulingam had been trapped by the authorities in the village of Caruniapuram. Some stories that circulated about the event broke her heart, for they said the police had subdued him, beaten him in their rage, and then shot him through the head. Edith Naish had been in the village when it happened but knew only that Jambulingam was indeed dead.

Remembering his pledge not to die with blood on his hands, Amy had to ask her, "Did he die clean?"

"Yes. He could have surely used his gun to kill, but he did not."

Over the next weeks Amy was very troubled by his death. She hoped the police would clear his name. Instead, they insisted it was good riddance to an evil man. One police official sneered that Amy would be very disappointed if she expected to see Jambulingam in heaven. Even after she

had written the story of Jambulingam in the book *Raj, Brig-
and Chief* and learned that many Indians were inspired to
come to Christ because of the conversion of Jambulingam,
she felt little better. She was haunted by the police official's
claim that Jambulingam had not been saved. Then on December 15, the evening before her fifty-sixth birthday, she
was resting in her room and enjoying the words of a hymn
sung by others in the dining room. Suddenly she was
flooded in waves of light. Her spirit soared. The Lord had
washed away her darkness, her doubt.

She murmured, "Jambulingam is—to use one of his favorite expressions—with 'Immanuel my help.' "[1]

Workers from Ireland and the British Isles continued
to arrive. One family—the Neills—was so gifted, it seemed
too good to be true. Husband and wife were both doctors.
They came about the same time as another doctor, May
Powell. At long last, Dohnavur had real doctors. Amy had
always maintained strict hygiene in the compound—which
helped to explain why there had never been one case of
cholera—but, oh, how they needed real doctors.

The Neills's son Stephen had been at Cambridge studying for the clergy. He had not been ordained, but he was
thoroughly steeped in the doctrine of the Church of England. Amy, influenced by Robert Wilson, claimed no de-
nomination. Besides her love of Christ, she expressed her
beliefs as three principles. First was the divine inspiration of
Scripture. Second was the power of prayer to enlist God's
help against the Enemy. Third was the necessity of the faithful to love one another. In the spirit of Keswick, Amy cared
nothing for doctrinal hairsplitting. The Lord's divine sum-
mation of *all* holiness was in the twenty-second chapter of
Matthew:

*Thou shalt love the Lord thy God with all thy heart,
and with all thy soul, and with all thy mind. This is
the first and great commandment. And the second is
like unto it, Thou shalt love thy neighbour as thyself.
On these two commandments hang all the law and
the prophets.*

The church service that had evolved from Amy's beliefs
was partly Anglican, partly Quaker, partly other churches, if
one had to use labels. Amy did not. But Stephen Neill did.
He labeled Amy one of the "Plymouth Brethren." Stephen's
mother asked, "Since Amy often has services led by those not
ordained, why shouldn't Stephen—by far the most qualified
—take over the services?" Slowly but surely, maintained the
mother, Stephen would steer the wayward services back to
the purity of Church of England ritual.

What had seemed so providential became chaos from
Amy's standpoint. Stephen Neill—prodded by his mother
—was virtually aspiring to be the "bishop" of Dohnavur.
The father and mother were trying to get Amy to agree to
have all medical facilities at a separate locale—under their
supervision, of course. Besides that, the father was spending far too much time with the girls at Dohnavur. This kind
of relationship was anathema to the Hindus. It could stain
Dohnavur. Then Stephen harangued Amy to launch a
sports program to send the boys and girls out into the villages. The Neills were truly brilliant people and they expected their brilliance to be given free rein. But Amy had
cautiously built Dohnavur into an oasis island of Christianity in a vast ocean of Hindus and Muslims.

"Lord, save me," said Amy, then wrote in her diary that
"the spiritual fortunes of the work hung by a thread."[2]

When she opposed all the Neills's programs, which she felt were undermining the security of Dohnavur, the Neills were stung by her "fear," her "insecurity." She was a myth, they whispered, trying to keep control of something that had grown far beyond her competence. But Amy persisted against the Neills. They dug in. They were not quitters. Brilliance would triumph. But Amy knew this competition for power could not continue. After six months of turmoil, she informed the Neills they must leave Dohnavur. And so they did, much of the conflict remaining secret and untold, the wounds never healing.

The conflict ushered in a new era for Dohnavur.

Amy officially severed all ties with missionary societies, though she had long thought her independence had been understood, even by her Zenana Missionary Society. After all, she always declared the society was not responsible for any debts she might incur. But after the Neills tried to wrestle Dohnavur away from her, she knew that stronger, more legalistic measures were required to protect her work. The Zenana Missionary Society had become more and more intrusive, too, demanding written reports as to what she planned to do, as to what she planned to spend, and answers to dozens of other questions. Perhaps she hadn't had one of her beloved colleagues smeared, as William Carey's Joshua Marshman had been back in the late 1820s, but her similarities to Carey were startling. They both had come to India with nothing, not even a formal education. They both had built up a large mission over decades. They both were passing into old age yet expected to provide accountability to a distant society committee that could not possibly administer a mission. Well, she would do just what Carey had done.

"Enough! It's over!"

Over the next two years she crafted the Dohnavur Fellowship, whose prime purpose was always to the Cross. Her motto was 'The Cross is the attraction,' but devotion to it had to have a human purpose, too:

> To save children in moral danger; to train them to serve others; to succour the desolate and the suffering; to do anything that may be shown to be the will of our Heavenly Father, in order to make His love known, especially to the people of India.[3]

And who led the Fellowship, who made its plans?

> The Leader with the help of the Council shall direct the conduct of the Fellowship according to the plans that God shall reveal. It is agreed that the supreme authority is vested in the Unseen Leader, the Lord Jesus Christ, while the human leader seeks, in cooperation with the other members, to carry out the mind and will of the Divine.[4]

The council consisted of eight of the best-qualified helpers. Of course Arulai was one. As far as qualifications to help at Dohnavur, Amy had only a list of about twenty-five questions she liked to ask volunteers. They were thoughtful questions with no right answers. Her hope was that the persons, in answering the questions, would be able to decide themselves whether they were fit for service or not. Some of the questions were:

> Samuel Rutherford said that there are some who would have Christ cheap, Christ "without the Cross.

But the price will not come down." Will you pay the price to live a crucified life?

Are you warmed or repelled by the thought of a hard life?

Do you know the Dohnavur Fellowship is a Family, not an institution? Are you willing to do whatever job helps the Family the most?

Besides the Bible, which three or four books have helped you the most?

Besides reading books, what activity refreshes you best when tired?

These questions were designed to ferret out any doubts that the volunteer might have. Not the least troubling was the very real possibility of spending as long as two years learning Tamil, for this necessity could not be shirked. Nor could the necessity to do whatever work was required, no matter how menial or tedious or perhaps even revolting. Hopefully she would not get people with their own ideas of what needed to be done. And certainly never again would she get people who came to Dohnavur to straighten out her mission!

The Dohnavur Fellowship had to become a legal entity, too. The mission society took the news like a lamb. They donated all property to the Dohnavur Fellowship. Buildings and land were being acquired all the time. In July 1925, Amy had purchased sixty acres of rocky hillside halfway between Dohnavur and Neyyoor. She called the spot "Three Pavilions," because legend said three ancient kings had conferred there. Also in 1925, she launched a project she had cherished for a long time: a house of prayer. It would be Indian in architecture, pagoda-like with tiles and multiple eaves, certainly not the foreign-looking Church of England style with stained-glass windows that so offended Indians. Amy had an aversion to images of the Lord anyway, so few were ever found in Dohnavur. The Cross was the image of Christ she wanted to see. The only other symbol in the House of Prayer was a large brass-rimmed wagon wheel. To Amy the wheel symbolized the Fellowship, an instrument to perform good hard work. The polished brass rim represented the bond of love that held the Fellowship together.

"And let's try hard to keep our furry and feathery friends out," she said of the squirrels, monkeys, and birds of Dohnavur she usually welcomed. "They will find no refuge in our church."

By 1926, there were seventy boys at Dohnavur. It was obvious they needed a strong leader. Arul Dasan was willing but lacked education. For that matter, new leadership for the entire Dohnavur Fellowship would have to come eventually. Amy was now fifty-nine. And there was the hospital she so desired. Few things attracted natives better than medical facilities. She had put the main thrust for a hospital aside until her House of Prayer was finished. But where were the doctors going to come from? Would the Neills poison all future attempts to attract doctors? Praise God, Dr. May Powell had remained, even though she was often bogged down in her study of Tamil. But even when Dr. Powell hit her stride, Dohnavur needed a male doctor for male patients. Indians would accept nothing else. Women doctors must examine girls. Men doctors must examine boys. All these things Amy now prayed for.

Dr. Godfrey Webb-Peploe had visited in 1925, but he had moved on to fulfill his commitments in China. Then in January 1926, his mother and his brother Murray, also a doctor, visited Dohnavur. Murray was the extrovert, Godfrey quiet and withdrawn. Both were steady and dedicated physicians. The brothers were grandsons of a very prominent speaker at the Keswick meetings. The old Reverend Mr. Webb-Peploe had won Amy's heart when he spoke of the joy of the Holy Spirit.

"Joy is not gush," he said emphatically. "Joy is not jolliness. Joy is perfect acquiescence in God's will."[5]

Amy found in Murray a soul mate. He was just as spontaneous as she was. If she heard the call to go somewhere, Murray was always ready to go with her. Off they would rumble in the Fellowship automobile! Murray was devout, too. He carried a well-worn New Testament in Greek and liked nothing better than to savor the Word.

After Murray departed with his mother for China in May 1926, Amy was torn. "My heart turns to him as Thy chosen leader for the hospital," she admitted to God in her diary. "I see in him and in Godfrey my very heart's desire." But guilt overwhelmed her. "Let me not covet my neighbor's goods—nor his manservants. Murray and Godfrey are China's manservants. Lord, help and forgive me."[6]

Still, she plunged ahead with her plans for the boys' compound. In September, she made a down payment on the land. Amy was in turmoil over the lack of a leader for the boys, writing in her diary the very next day, "It is as if the evil one were seeking to undermine what he failed to overthrow by open assault, our perfect unity."[7] But one week later she received a cable that was like a monsoon of joy. Godfrey and his mother were returning to Dohnavur! Godfrey had a touch of lung trouble and had been ordered to leave China until he felt better. Once again, Amy had to scold herself. She must not take joy in China's loss. But how could she stop her own hopes for India? And when Godfrey told her he had resigned his post in China, her heart soared.

Godfrey soon set her straight. "Don't count on me for Dohnavur," he said morosely.

Lord, how could she have been so selfish? So foolish? So presumptuous? Did Godfrey see Dohnavur as nothing more than a pleasant diversion while he was recuperating? Yet when Godfrey returned to Dohnavur, Amy felt sure God had been telling her that sober, steady Godfrey was her future leader for the boys, her future doctor for the hospital. How could she have been so wrong?

On December 15, 1926, the evening before her fifty-ninth birthday, she got the best present she could possibly get. A note from Godfrey asked Amy for fellowship in Dohnavur. And his note revealed what had been troubling him. He had doubted he was worthy of what she expected of him. Yes, he was a doctor, but could he lead the boys? At last he had decided he must try. Amy had that effect on people. She made Godfrey want very much to be what she thought he was.

Godfrey tackled Tamil and was so adept at it he had a working knowledge of it by the time his health was back to normal. Then he assumed all the duties Amy had bestowed upon him. To make the Webb-Peploe saga even more miraculous, Murray's station at Hangchow was overrun in 1927 by the Chinese civil war. Murray had to flee to Dohnavur. But he assured Amy he had every intention of returning to China when the shooting was over. Again, Amy had a call from God to proceed boldly. In January 1928, she bought the land for the hospital.

It seemed hopeless to defy Amy's plans, which were responses to God's call. By July 1928, Murray, too, had pledged to the Dohnavur Fellowship. With Godfrey in charge of the boys' compound, it was left to Murray to ramrod the construction of the new hospital. It would require the most funds they had ever committed. Even the children worked to raise funds. They picked berries from the margosa tree and sold buckets of them for oil. And the children tried many other moneymaking projects.

Southern India was not a hot spot for the politics that were sweeping northern India. But Amy followed what was happening. Mohandas Gandhi was in and out of jail. His nationalist movement, embodied in peaceful resistance to British rule, was now called *satyagraha,* or "force of truth." Often, Gandhi would appear to be doing nothing, then suddenly surface in a cauldron of unrest.

One event in 1930 not only consolidated native resistance but shocked the world. The British taxed salt, which affected every Indian, no matter how poor. In protest, Gandhi led a march of Indians to the sea, where they could make their own salt. Of course, the British arrested the "troublemaker" and threw him into jail. This time Gandhi's followers had enough courage to push ahead without him. Nearly twenty-five hundred Indians marched on the government's huge salt pans at Dharasana, north of Bombay. They intended to occupy the pans, but British officers ordered police to attack them with metal-tipped *lathis.* Hundreds of unresisting marchers fell with cracked skulls. Journalists witnessed and reported the scene, which was so ghastly and inhuman that it seemed impossible.

"The heavy-handed British rule of India is an outrage," said Amy. "When will it end?"

Yet the way of the Hindus was harsh, too. Amy's bold *Things As They Are* had at long last been confirmed by another writer, an American. Katherine Mayo's *Mother India,* published in 1927, was a shocker. Yes, girl babies were often offered to the gods, she confirmed. Once abandoned at the river's edge, they now were neglected unto death or sold to temples. Not only were the young girls terribly degraded, but many actually died from physical acts they were far too young to perform. Amy had borne the ridicule of an unbelieving world to save temple children. Now Katherine Mayo acknowledged Amy's work in her book as "extraordinary."

The last few years had been fruitful for Dohnavur. The House of Prayer was finished. Development of the boys' compound was underway. The hospital was started. Although it would take many years to complete, in 1929 Murray performed what Amy called his "first big spectacular operation"![18] Eventually there would be a prayer room above the operating theater. But during that first surgery Amy had the entire family in the House of Prayer petitioning God for success. For two hours they prayed and sang—two minutes it seemed to Amy—before a messenger came to tell them the result of the operation.

"Praise God for that success!"

The leadership Amy had prayed for was now in place. In January 1931, she gathered together many of her helpers to confide in them. Did it not seem God wanted Murray to head the hospital effort? Yes. Did it not seem God wanted Godfrey not only to doctor but to lead the boys, too? Yes. And Amy was now sure God wanted May Powell to lead the girls. No one disagreed.

The Fellowship branched out beyond Dohnavur. This was not itinerant evangelizing but a serious effort to establish permanent facilities, initiated by medical dispensaries. Four miles to the northwest they were taking root in Kalakadu, a stronghold of Hindus. Two miles south they entered Eruvadi, a Muslim stronghold.

The Saturday morning of October 24, 1931, Amy prayed, "Do anything, Lord, that will fit me to serve Thee and help my beloveds."[9]

In Kalakadu, her helpers had secured a house that was supposedly haunted. It would carry Christ's Cross. Two of the Fellowship would be stationed there, led by May Parker. Amy had visited it on October 9, noting work being done on the bathing shed. The following week she visited Eruvadi. Things were proceeding smoothly. This Saturday, she went once again to Eruvadi. Even though it was late in the afternoon, she decided to go with two Sitties to visit Kalakadu again. So the driver chugged the automobile over to Kalakadu. Amy left the car and approached the house in dimming twilight. Off to the side was the shed that would shelter their outdoor toilet. Had they dug the pit yet? Perhaps she should check.

Then Amy tumbled into the center of the earth!

THIRTEEN

A my writhed in the freshly dug earth.

She was at the bottom of a pit, which had been dug where she hadn't expected it. Her hands clutched the sandy soil to fight the pain in her ankle. It was severely sprained, perhaps broken. But where was help? Where were the Sitties? Where was her driver? Where were the villagers, who had always scrutinized the activity at the house since the Fellowship began renovating it? She clawed up the walls of her pit to get upright, taking care to keep weight off the injured ankle. Upright, she felt joy. Praise God she had not broken her neck. Hands suddenly lifted her from the pit and gently stretched her out.

"Thank you," she said in Tamil.

"The demon struck you down, memsahib," said a man in awe.

Why argue? Maybe it was true. She spotted her driver among the faces. "Please get word to Dohnavur I've had an accident," she groaned.

"Right away!"

Tears streamed down the faces of Amy's Sitties. "Praise God this did not happen to May Parker," she comforted them.

The pain grew. Two hours later, May Powell arrived in a truck. Now Amy understood as never before what the appearance of medical help meant to these Indians. Medical people seemed absolutely angelic. And how the Lord must love these willing workers. By now her ankle felt like a great melon, the skin about to burst.

After a few minutes of examination, May Powell said, "We must take you to Neyyoor. The ankle must be X-rayed at the London Mission Society Hospital."

So off into the black night they rumbled the forty-six miles to Neyyoor on a "road" built up between rice paddies. Ronald Proctor drove the truck. May Powell and Mary Mills, a nurse, comforted Amy during the bumpy ride. Rain was making the road even more treacherous. Once the truck shot across a washout, hurling every passenger into the air as it struck the other side. Amy's injuries were battered even more. Yet it seemed a miracle the truck did not overturn into a flooded field. It was Sunday evening by the time the ankle was X-rayed in Neyyoor. Howard Somervell, the fearless missionary who had helped Amy rescue a girl more than thirty years before, was one of the doctors who attended her. Amy was being prepared for surgery. The anesthesiologist was holding the ether mask. Amy had learned her leg was broken above the ankle.

"How long before I'm walking about again?" asked Amy.

Doctor Somervell said, "The ankle must be in splints for eight weeks. Let us pray: 'Oh, Lord, make this ankle strong enough to bear burdens again.' "

Oh yes. Amy prayed, too. The mask for the ether was put on her face. Psalm 6 expressed her concern perfectly: "Have mercy upon me, O LORD; for I am weak: O LORD, heal me; for my bones are vexed." But wait. Had the good doctor evaded her question? He hadn't actually said she would be walking, had he?

The next day, Amy groaned involuntarily as the pain-numbing morphine wore off. "If only I could take your pain from you," sighed Mary Mills.

Amy blurted, "Your joy no man taketh from you."

God's words from Scripture had just come to her, as they so often did. With Mary's help, the passage was found in the sixteenth chapter of the book of John:

> *A woman when she is in travail hath sorrow, be-*
> *cause her hour is come: but as soon as she is delivered*
> *of the child, she remembereth no more the anguish,*
> *for joy that a man is born into the world. And ye*
> *now therefore have sorrow: but I will see you again,*
> *and your heart shall rejoice, and your joy no man*
> *taketh from you.*

So there it was. This agony was the birth of some joy.

Back in Dohnavur, on November 3, the pain subsided, which allowed her doctors to wean Amy off the morphine. Too much use was habit-forming. But then the pain returned. And it grew in intensity. The ache remained day after day. Then week after week. Was the ankle not mending properly? Was it infected? In any event the pain robbed her of her sleep. Amy spent her sixty-fourth birthday in her room, quite unable to do anything but lie in bed and try to read, though her mind was befuddled and exhausted from lack of sleep. Her visitors were allowed a mere fifteen seconds to wish her well. The others began to sense that the injuries were much worse than voiced by the doctors.

On Christmas Day, carols were sung outside her room. On January 4, 1932, the council requested three solid hours of prayer by the Fellowship. Amy actually did seem to improve. She was well enough to be transported about in the automobile to survey various projects. When Dr. Somervell visited in February, he seemed satisfied with her progress. But sometimes she felt she was not mending well at all. Had inactivity allowed the years of unceasing toil to catch up with the Musal?

In July she confessed in a letter, "Sometimes I think the kind of tiredness that comes after such years as those that lie behind could never be rested anywhere but There."[1] What an admission. No real rest until Paradise!

But usually she was as convinced as everyone else she was on the mend. Every advance was noted. Six steps one day. Ten steps another day. Went for a drive in the automobile. Walked out on the verandah. Walked down the steps to the prayer room. This great accomplishment was just before her sixty-fifth birthday. She certainly didn't waste her time, even though she had not one night of real sleep since the accident. For a long time, friends had urged her to write a history of Dohnavur. Besides being an artist with words, only Amy had the knowledge to readily synthesize such an enormous amount of activity. Yes, it was all recorded but scattered in eighteen books and thousands of letters.

"So I will weave all the stories together as the *Gold Cord*," she promised.

As if Amy didn't have enough to do, she now pecked

out on the typewriter the *Daily Manna* for distribution within the Fellowship. The creation of this daily spiritual aid was of course spurred by the fact that she could not circulate to mother her flock as she had done for so many years. She expressed her lament once to Murray. "I do pray to be out of bonds at least so as to be able to be at meals and about the house. I think many trials of various kinds could be avoided if only the Family could be a bit more 'mothered.' After all, it's a mere matter of 'buffering,' spiritual 'buffering.'"[2]

An example of her spiritual buffering in the *Daily Manna* read:

> *Have we any prayer like "use me, O Lord" in the Bible? . . . [No] I could not find any such prayer. . . [I] find every other verb occurring in prayer—teach me, lead me, bless me, and so on—but not this verb which we would naturally expect. . . . The Captain will use the soldier if he be prepared for use; words of beseeching on the soldier's part are not required. . . .[3]*

The next day in the *Daily Manna* she expanded her thoughts:

> *I have three pens, one for ordinary writing, one a little finer, and one for fine work like corrections. . . . The pens are always ready for use, "very usable." Even so, just as a fountain pen is all the better for being some-times left under water, so our souls do often need to be bathed afresh in the love of God. . . And we are given one day in seven for something of this sort. . . .[4]*

The *Daily Manna* by no means replaced the very

personal letters she sent to individuals in the compound. About this time she wrote:

> *All our love flows from His heart of love. We are like little pools on the rocks of Joppa. You know how we have watched the great sea washing over them and flooding them till they overflow. That is what the love of God does for us. We have no love ourselves. . . .* [5]

The year 1932 also saw the Indian struggle against British domination continue. Gandhi—now called the Mahatma, or "great soul"—and thirty-five thousand others of the National Congress were imprisoned. Confusing nearly everyone, Gandhi protested the British announcement that they would allow the Untouchable caste to hold their own separate elections so that they could have representatives in the provincial legislatures. Gandhi said if this were done, he would starve himself to death in prison!

"Gandhi believes the British will institutionalize the Untouchables with this supposedly generous gesture," someone explained.

In fact, Gandhi railed against discrimination of Untouchables by Hindus. Still, one could never be sure what Gandhi would do next. He seemed utterly original. In his unpredictable way, he said he didn't care a whit for what he had said twenty years before; he cared only for truth. He knew the Sermon on the Mount by heart. He would startle onlookers by leading them in his favorite Christian hymn, "Lead Kindly Light." He anguished that Hindus were so hidebound they would prevent someone from killing a rabid dog. Yet Gandhi, himself of the Vaisya caste, defended much of Hinduism. He fathomed the complexities of Hindu society, and he didn't want India to collapse into chaos. Most Indians knew little of his actual politics. The only thing everyone knew about him was that when he was free, he drew immense crowds. Tens of thousands. Indians believed he was the one authority who cared if they lived or died. The only thing the British knew was that if he starved himself to death in prison, the Indians might rebel. And no matter how repressive and brutal the British were, outnumbered one thousand to one, they could not withstand a full rebellion!

Although Amy's pain and sleepless nights continued, she seemed to improve. How could she dare think otherwise? She even took trips to the Gray Jungle. She felt so invigorated on one trip that she tried to run on the verandah of the Forest House. But then she began to get worse. Her left hand numbed into a useless thing. The sight in one eye deteriorated. Arthritis stung her with every breath, especially in her back. Oh, how she thought she would die in harness. But no, her fate seemed the worst possible.

"Do not, I beseech Thee, let me be disabled by pain or inability and live on as a burden to others," she had written after a nightmare many years previous.

Now the nightmare was all true. She began to hate her spacious room, which had a sign over one door that said "Room of Peace." It was originally intended to be a room where several of the Fellowship might sleep. It was never intended to be the sumptuous room of the pampered queen bee. It even had a teakwood partition, deemed important now that she was almost invalid. When visitors entered the room through blue curtains—what other color would Amy choose?—they saw no bed, only the partition on the right and bookcases on the left. Straight ahead were large windows onto the wide verandah. On the best of days blue kingfishers could be seen knifing down into huge vessels full of minnows.

There was a desk there, too, with a wicker-backed chair. Amy had her reminders posted. Most prominent was "God hath not given us the spirit of fear." The bookcases were filled with all of her favorites. Besides writing the *Gold Cord* at the desk and her normal correspondence, Amy was also writing about her illness. Many letters were to other invalids, a group eventually deemed the "Dohnavur Invalids' League." Some letters were cranky, all were seeking the why of sickness. Eventually she decided she might collect all these letters into a book for sick people. As a metaphor for getting good from the birthing pain, she titled it *Rose from Brier.* It would be unique in that it was written by a sick person to other sick people. She composed the sentiment in four lines:

> *The toad beneath the harrow knows*
> > *Exactly where each tooth-point goes;*
> *The butterfly upon the road*
> > *Preaches contentment to that toad.*[6]

No, this book was not written by the unaffected butterfly but by the battle-weary toad. Oh, if only her little *Rose from Brier* could be to one person what *The Pilgrim's Progress* was to her:

> *There are books. . .that we could not do without. (How glad I would be if the little "Rose" might be that, even to only one.) Among mine I name very gratefully* The Pilgrim's Progress. *I do not think that we find the gathered wealth of truth and power and beauty in that book till we read it after life has had time to explain it. . . .*[7]

Amy became more pensive, more meditative than ever. Her Bible study led her to resolve to enter into this torture heart and soul. Yet she was reluctant to admit illness made prayer easier. Still, one night "after neuritis had taken possession" of her "from shoulder blade to finger tips," a "prayer, so simple, so easy for a tired heart, had a delivering power."[8] She thought much about prayer. She noted "the gates of access into the Father's presence are open continually. There is no need to push—perhaps 'trying to pray' is sometimes a sort of pushing."[9] She was startled by the thought that at times she might be working more in the Lord's will as an invalid than she did as Amy the Musal. And she wrote:

> Is it not worth our while to call a halt and ask the question? Are we so busy with our multiform labours of philanthropy and love that we have no time to stop and think? India can show a missionary army of hard-working men and women. Go where you will throughout this land, you will find the Christian workers incessantly busy at their work... No charge of idleness can be made against us, as a whole. But how is it that so much of our busy energy appears to be expended in vain? Holy Scripture, personal experience, the voice of conscience, all these alike suggest one answer—we have neglected largely the means which God Himself has ordained for anointing from on High....[10]

Prayer!
Amy was certain that the weakness of their prayers was the reason heathenism still enslaved the Indians. How could missionaries neglect the greatest source of help from

God? The Lord certainly had not neglected prayer in the Gospels. So Amy formulated discourses on prayer, noting that it all meant nothing unless put into practice:

1. *Don't get into bondage about place, or position of the body. . .sometimes, at least, [Our Lord] went into the open air to a hillside; to a garden. . .I have known some who could kneel hours by a chair. . . walking up and down; this was Bishop Moule's way. Some go into their rooms and shut the door. . . . Let the leaning of your mind lead you; a God-directed mind leans to what helps the spirit most. . . .*

2. *Don't be discouraged if at first you seem to get nowhere. . .no command in the Bible [is] so difficult to obey and so penetrating in power. . .[as] "Be still and know that I am God." Many have found this so. . . .*

3. *Don't feel it is necessary to pray all the time; listen. . . . And read the Words of Life. Let them enter into you.*

4. *Don't forget there is one other person interested in you—extremely interested. . .there is no truer word than the old couplet:*
   Satan trembles when he sees
   The weakest saint upon his knees.

5. *Don't give up in despair if no thoughts and no words come, but only distractions and inward confusions. Often it helps to use the words of others. . . Psalm, hymn, song—use what helps most.*

6. *Don't worry if you fall to sleep. "He giveth unto His beloved in sleep."*

7. *And if the day ends in what seems failure, don't*
    fret. Tell Him you're sorry. Even so, don't be dis-
    couraged. All discouragement is of the devil. . . .[11]

Another time she noted three more things about
prayer:

1. *We don't need to explain to our Father things*
    that are known to Him.
2. *We don't need to press Him, as if we had to deal*
    with an unwilling God.
3. *We don't need to suggest to Him what to do, for*
    He Himself knows what to do.[12]

Of a group prayer meeting in her room at the Forest
House in October 1933, Amy said, "There are many in our
family who come to prayer meetings because it is the custom
to do so, but who are not urged by a great desire. It is the lack
of prayer-hunger that often makes a big united meeting difficult."[13] Soon after she expressed the opinion her pain became so great she could no longer be present in group prayer
meetings. Her unrelieved agony was too great a distraction
for the others.

Oh, Lord, had that meeting in the Forest House been
her last?

FOURTEEN

A few months later in Dohnavur, one thoughtful council member suggested that they routinely assemble in Amy's Room of Peace before their general meeting to pray with her.

"That quarter of an hour was like one long drink of cold water on a hot day!"[1] Amy gasped in appreciation.

Amy's surroundings were improved by the addition of a spacious bird habitat, more an aviary than a cage, on the verandah. But to her nurse's consternation, she often allowed some of the birds into her room. Her Room of Peace now also displayed Doctor Somervell's oil painting of Nanga Parbat, the most treacherous peak in the Himalayas. No one had ever managed to reach the summit. Many had died trying. Somervell was a climber of renown himself. Nanga Parbat was an old foe. But to Amy, Somervell would never reach greater heights than he had in rescuing a child from temple prostitution thirty years before. Every day was a mountain for

Somervell. At Neyyoor, in 1931, she had heard him being called to administer medicine hour after hour, rarely able to sleep, slogging on always to one more patient.

She continued to write—had she ever been more productive than when she was an invalid? In 1934, she told her publisher—which since 1928 had been the Society for the Promotion of Christian Knowledge—about her latest book *Ploughed Under,* "A book is a child. . .I want the book thin. I don't like podgy books. . .don't let my little lover come out fat. . . ."[2]

Godfrey had written the *Dohnavur Letter* for a couple of years. But in 1933, Amy added a second newsletter called *Dust of Gold.* It was in that new creation that she wrote:

> *Pray that every book, booklet, letter, that goes out*
> *from this Fellowship may have blood and iron in it.*
> *Pray that we may never degenerate to the merely in-*
> *teresting, the pretty. . . .*[3]

The return, in June 1935, of Murray from his furlough in Australia—he came back with wife Oda and two new twin boys—did not bolster her spirits as she had anticipated. By this time she began to suspect the worst: She was not going to recover. Was the Musal dead? She had rested for more than three years and was in more pain now than when she fell into the pit.

Well, what had she expected? She expressed it in a poem for *Toward Jerusalem,* another book she was working on:

> *Hast thou no scar?*
> *No hidden scar on foot, or side, or hand?*
> *I hear thee sung as mighty in the land,*

I hear them hail thy bright, ascendant star,
Hast thou no scar?

Hast thou no wound?
    Yet I was wounded by the archers, spent,
Leaned Me against a tree to die; and rent
    By ravening beasts that compassed Me, I
    swooned:
Hast thou no wound?

No wound? No scar?
    Yet, as the Master shall the servant be,
And pierced are the feet that follow Me;
    But thine are whole: can he have followed far
Who has nor wound nor scar?[4]

Her growing state of mind was only too clear in July 1934, when upon hearing one of the doctors say she probably had only five years left of her earthly existence, she dropped him a note the next day:

I wonder if ever before you made anyone so happy
with just a few words. . . . I know He might even
now ask for longer than that five years, but that
there is even a natural hope of that little while being
enough, is purest joy. Last night I lay awake too
happy to sleep. . . . Only pray that He will "take
from me all slothfulness that I may fill up the
crevices of my time," and truly finish all He wants
me to do. . . .[5]

And yet at other times—her Gethsemanes—she longed

to recover and had to write, "O Lord, forgive... Canst Thou not deliver me from the strivings of my longings to be well and with my Family again? But a thousand, thousand thanks to Thee for their longsuffering love, for everything. . . ."[6]

Her thoughts on prayer continued to evolve. On her sixty-eighth birthday in 1935 she wrote:

> To pray alone, without the uplifting wings of music and the warm fellow-feeling of others like-minded is I think, a very stripping thing. Nothing but bare prayer is left you, prayer stripped to the bone; and you learn, sometimes with dismay, how little you know of real prayer. At least that is how it often is with me. . . .[7]

Godfrey's duties finally became so crushing and Amy was doing so well with *Dust of Gold* that the *Dohnavur Letter* was discontinued. But Amy's health was not improving. By February 27, 1935, she was recording, "Yesterday a very low day. Read Samuel Rutherford."[8] From 1931 to 1935, she had been carried up to her precious Gray Jungle every September. But after 1935, this trip was deemed too strenuous for her. So, in hot weather, Amy would now have to suffer the sizzling summer heat.

She battled self-pity. In spite of her productive writing, she was isolated. And pain never left her. In 1936 she wrote a prayer, "My Lord and my Beloved, I thank Thee for holding off the sharpness of the pain and longing this evening. I can even hear them singing without crushing back the tears. This is the first time it has been so. . . ."

Again and again she caught herself yearning to be mobile again. When she heard children were being taken on their first trip up into the Gray Jungle, she wrote, "I was longing to see their pleasure as they see it for the first time. . .when suddenly I remembered that I shall see them when for the first time they look at the loveliness *There* (heaven). I shall be *There* to show them everything. . . ."[10]

Her earlier petition to spare her from "slothfulness" was not an empty plea. For many months, her strength, her desire ebbed. Amy realized a real need to record the development of the Dohnavur Fellowship since *Gold Cord*, published in 1932. So she had started this needed work, which she titled *Windows*, but the strength to pull all the information together just wasn't there. Such a compilation was much more taxing than a poignant story like *Mimosa*. *Mimosa* had been a sensation. Since 1924 it had appeared in nine languages besides English. Letters of appreciation came to Amy from all over the world. And even after her accident, she had written *Ploughed Under*, the story of Arulai. No, a compilation like *Windows* was hard to do. So she set it aside. She soothed her regret over it by reminding herself God knew when things had to be done. Suddenly one morning in July 1936, for the first time in eight months, power came to her. She worked on *Windows* thirteen hours a day for three days!

"I can't account for it by any rational means," she shrugged. "Nothing else was different."

Her strength fired up again in late 1936. Another story, as poignant as *Mimosa* or *Ploughed Under*, had to be told. This one she would call *Kohila*, for the beautiful curly-headed child who first came to Dohnavur in 1913, then had to be exiled for a while. Kohila was darling but had a spitfire temper. Once she had refused to share her room, clinging to it like a tiger. But once in Christ, no one shared more or worked harder. Soon she had been singing the little workers' song:

> I scrub my pots, I scrub my pans,
>   I scrub my brasses and my cans,
> I sweep and scrub each red floor tile
>   Till I can see it smile.
> And as I scrub I feel so gay
>   It might be my own Coming-Day;
> For work is such a jolly thing
>   It makes one want to sing.[11]

Maturity of several more years brought Kohila real passion:

> Give me a passionate passion for souls,
>   Give me a pity that yearns,
> Give me the love that loves unto death,
>   Give me the fire that burns,
> Give me, O Lord, to be fervent in prayer,
>   Pouring out all for the lost;
> Give me to pray in the Conqueror's Name,
>   Spirit of Pentecost.[12]

Kohila grew into a woman of great commitment to Christ. Few worked harder. She had become a head nurse at the Place of Healing. It was the custom at Dohnavur to decorate a person's room with flowers on her Coming Day. Kohila had always relished this gesture. One of her best friends was soon to have a Coming Day. Up in the Gray Jungle, Kohila knew of gorgeous purple flowers, extraprecious because they grew on a high rocky slope and were difficult to get. As she climbed after them, she slipped and fell, and at the age of twenty-eight, Kohila was dead.

Arulai consoled Amy, "You must press the love of God close against yourself. That's the only way to buffer the pain of this dreadful loss."

Yes, Amy had to write this story called *Kohila*. In it she also wrote more extensively than she ever had before of spiritual training. "The thing the devil most fears is prayer!"[13] she insisted, never neglecting her favorite weapon.

But necessity taken care of, Amy's strength would wane again. And worse, her pain would increase. On November 9, 1937—her special anniversary day of coming to India back in 1895—she was too much in pain to see anyone. Still, she gave God thanks when Mary Mills, her "perfect nurse," said everyone in the Fellowship prayed for Amy in the House of Prayer. It was a time like that when she worried most about her successors. Oh yes, the Webb-Peploe brothers and May Powell were in place. Of them she prayed on November 14, 1937, "And once more I thank Thee for those who are doing everything so perfectly now."[14] But the three were physicians —and Europeans. Amy firmly believed Europeans should be behind the scenes, never in front. "India can be best reached by Indians,"[15] she had always maintained. But where was the Indian leadership?

There should have been little concern in her mind. After Ponnammal passed away, Arulai was the natural choice for Indian leadership. In *Ploughed Under*, published in 1934, Amy declared of Arulai, "She has shared in every part of the work from the beginning. . . . To me no word so perfectly describes her as the great word *loyal*. Her faithful heart has never swerved. . . ."[16]

For many years, Amy was certain that Arulai was to be

the eventual leader of the women's side of the work at Dohnavur. Her Tamil was good. Her English was good. She read the New Testament and the Septuagint version of the Old Testament in Greek. She was very discerning of the qualities of Sitties and Accals. And she had compassion. The only question was her health, and it had begun to fail in 1935. Though Arulai seemed to bounce back, Amy was worried. And before the year 1938 was out, Arulai's valiant younger sister, Mimosa, died.

"Not yet fifty years old," grieved an anxious Amy.

Then in the early days of 1939, Arulai's health failed again. It was not languor, nor weakness, but a precipitous decline. Soon she, too, was an invalid. Amy and Arulai sent letters back and forth. Ironically, the doctors advised against either one visiting the other because of their fragile health. Yet it was Amy who reassured the doctors, "Be at rest about Arulai. She is perhaps the most precious thing I have on earth. . . . She has been the very joy of my heart, my utterly loyal child, and she is in His Hands who loves her more than I do. . . . It is the Trust of the Unexplained. . . ."[17]

When Arulai became gravely ill, Amy asked of her nurse, "Tell her that after I see His Face the first face I shall want to see will be hers, and for ever and for ever we shall be together again. . . ."[18]

On May 24, 1939, word came to Amy that Arulai was with Christ. Amy called all of Arulai's friends to her room and hugged them one by one. Tears were streaming down her face, but she assured them they were tears of joy. Because Amy was too feeble to attend Arulai's funeral in God's Garden, Arulai's nephew, Rajappan, stayed in Amy's room to comfort her. Together they read the Book of Revelation and the magnificent portion of *The Pilgrim's Progress* where Christian enters the Celestial City.

"What glory Arulai has entered!" enthused Rajappan, understanding that Amy's tears really were of joy.

"Perfection," murmured Amy.

It was no surprise that Amy wished fervently for her own "perfection."

FIFTEEN

In October 1938, Amy had said of a dream, "Is it imagi- nation, Lord, or Thine own word to me, that I shall come to Thee in sleep—no rending good-byes—no distress to anyone? . . . However it be, I ask that it may be the eas- iest way for my beloveds."[1] Her pampered queen-bee exis- tence gave her guilt. One month later she prayed, "Lord Jesus, Thou hast made my prison so beautiful and my bonds so light that I greatly fear I do not 'suffer with' Thee."[2]

Amy fought hard to subdue, even bury the self. On October 24, 1939, the eighth anniversary of the accident, she scolded the Fellowship:

> For eight years many of you have daily prayed for me, not the ordinary costless prayer. . .but something more vital. . . . From the depths of my heart I thank you. . . . I thought then that the bars would be broken. Every day I thought, "It will be tomorrow." The answer has

*come otherwise. . .[But] the world is so full of the
tremendous and prayer-compelling, that I don't want
you to spend one minute on me. . . .*[3]

But even dwelling on self in this vein made her feel
guilty. To remind herself how fortunate she was, Amy had
only to remember faithful Irene Streeter, who had recently
died in a plane crash. In 1939, Amy wrote to Olive Gib-
son, Irene's replacement as representative of the Fellowship
in England:

*Go gently. Don't do as I know I did, for truly I had to
do it. Don't work each day till you are unable to do one
minute more. Don't. Leave a margin. It doesn't matter
that I did it, for there are all these [the Webb-Peploe
brothers and May Powell] ready to take over. . .[but]
there is no one as yet preparing to [replace you]. . . .*[4]

Amy was at her best when mothering others. On December 7, 1939, she admonished some of the little ones:

*Oh my children, if only you would make up your
minds never to doubt the love of another sister or
brother in Christ, but always think the best, to take
the best for granted, and never admit an unkind
thought in your heart, how happy, how heavenly life
would be. I could not endure it if for one minute I
doubted any one of you. It would be like the sting of
a wasp in my soul. Why do you endure it? Why do
some of you even encourage that wasp to sting? I beseech you to have done with this. Refuse it. Hate it.
It may seem a trifle, but it is of hell. . . .*[5]

The sprawling Dohnavur grounds had long been inaccessible to Amy by walking. Only in her memory could she walk off her verandah to the nearby guest cottages, then beyond to the buildings that housed the weaving shed, the girls' dormitories, the medical dispensary, the girls' school, the milk kitchen, the many nurseries, the workrooms, and the House of Prayer. Certainly she would never ever make it to the hospital, the swimming pool, the playing fields, or the various boys' compounds. From north to south the complex stretched six hundred yards, from east to west even farther because the Place of Heavenly Healing was across the irrigation channel. The buildings must have covered one hundred acres. To think that she had watched it all spring up over thirty years.

"Flowers from God, prayed for and received."

Since the accident in 1931, Amy claimed to have had only eight nights of real sleep. Right after the accident she hardly slept at all and often read. For the first time she had tried a novel, something she previously dismissed as far too trivial. To her delight she found a novelist in harmony with her own thoughts: John Buchan. Buchan was a contemporary, a Scot. One of his sentences, "He asked of him the ultimate service, as a friend should,"[6] struck Amy as absolutely true. That was exactly what she had asked of Handley Bird, as well as others. A novel so true to real life, she decided, was not a waste of time but akin to reading poetry.

The events of late 1939 threatened even that tiny indulgence. Europe seemed headed toward another great war—not drifting but wildly careening. India's turmoil continued, too. Gandhi, who had hoped to "retire" into his spiritual pursuits, was forced into the fray again. He fasted in protest over a British agreement with the maharajah of Rajkot. The

British acquiesced, proving the old man still had more influence than any native leader in India. But this squabble soon paled next to world events. Germany—led by a dictator so demonic he seemed the Antichrist—began conquering Europe. Gandhi and the National Congress demanded that Britain state its war aims to the Indians. When Britain ignored the demand, the Hindu leaders insisted that this was one war in which Indians would not participate. But to further divide India, the Muslims declared their support for the British war effort.

"Looks rather grim," said the Webb-Peploes.

Britain plunged headlong into war against Germany. Three young men of the Fellowship went into the British army. Several of the Tamil youths went into the Indian armed forces. Murray suggested a Spiritual Civic Guard on the home front. Amy had mixed emotions:

> Can you even begin to imagine what it means to me that while I lie here like a slug on a cabbage leaf. . . you are strong and doing exploits? . . . You have the glorious double message to give—the certainty of the triumph of righteousness, whatever the sacrifice be, and the fact that all this turmoil is perhaps the last herald of the Coming of the King. . .[but] I mustn't get too hot over Spiritual Civics—it's just the heritage of my Scottish-Northern Irish blood. . . .[7]

Great strength was needed. How frustrated Amy became:

> In the last war [World War I], I could go about among you. . .like a mother bear whose cubs are

threatened. I felt strong to fight for you. Now [during
World War II] there is no strength at all. . .And
thoughts piled up as they do at night. . . . What if?
And the burden was heavy. And then it was if a
voice said almost aloud, "Leave it to Me, child,
leave it to Me." [8]

So she tended her flock. To one she wrote, "Sometimes I have been anxious about you because you have said, 'If you leave us I can't bear to go on.' That is all wrong, my darling. . . . You won't give way and fail. That would be utter defeat. I did not train you for anything so ignoble as defeat. . . ."[9]

In 1940, a pact among Germany, Italy, and Japan caused more fear in Asia. Japan, so near India, was very powerful militarily. On December 7, 1941, Japanese dive-bombers devastated the American naval fleet in the Pacific Ocean. This would keep Americans from helping any victims in Asia for a long while. The Japanese began aggression in earnest. They struck the Chinese in force. Later they attacked Burma, too, pushing the British out. Burma was India's neighbor.

On April 6, 1942, the Japanese bombed Madras!

"It seems India is in this war whether the 'Mahatma' likes it or not," commented some.

Dohnavur sensed the immediacy of the war. Evacuation plans were developed. If the Japanese invaded, everyone in the Fellowship under the age of thirty-five, now numbering more than three hundred, would proceed immediately to the Gray Jungle. But the Japanese attack on Madras was only a probe. The first great manifestation of the war was a famine in the area around Calcutta. But why? The

immense paddy lands of the Bengal had not failed the Indians in recent memory. Hundreds of thousands of fields were
scattered along immense rivers. The rice was delivered to the
millions in the cities in thousands of boats. But now country
people flocked into Calcutta, carrying everything they owned
in one basket or a box. "Where is the rice?" they cried.

Soon the tragedy was known. All boats had been req-
uisitioned by the British for the war effort. But what of the
Indian people? The catastrophe of 1943 seemed to prove
that the British didn't care if Indians lived or died. Everywhere in Bengal people starved. Mothers' milk dried up.
Babies died. The numbers of dead mounted. Ten thousand.
One hundred thousand. Finally, one million. Two million!
More. Mountains of smoke plumed into the air as Hindu
dead were burned in pyres along the rivers. Gandhi was imprisoned, silenced. No one spoke for the Indians. It was
some consolation to Amy to learn a recent estimate placed
the number of Christian Indians at seven million, an increase of four million in the last thirty years.

"Someday the British will be gone from India, but
Christ will remain," she prayed.

Amy labored the only way she could. She continued to
counsel, inform, scold, shepherd, and perform a dozen
other duties by writing. By 1943 she had once again up-
dated the history of the Dohnavur Fellowship, this time in
a book titled *Though the Mountains Shake*. So this book,
Things As They Are, Gold Cord, and *Windows* chronicled the
more than forty years of the Dohnavur effort. *Though the
Mountains Shake* also included the wrenching account of
Arulai's death.

The disaster in India worsened on December 5, 1943.
Explosions shattered the silence in Calcutta. Yet the

bombing of Calcutta was just another probe by the Japanese, followed by nothing. After that bombing raid, life actually began to improve for the Indians. Britain was more sensitive to their needs. Although the boats were needed in the war effort, they nevertheless delivered rice again. One of the greatest famines in the history of the world ended, seemingly no more than a footnote in the worst war in the history of the world.

SIXTEEN

A sia for Asians!" cried many Indians.

Some Indians were so bitter they joined Japanese armies in Burma. Japan sensed that 1944 was the right time to conquer India. In March they bombed airfields in the Naga Hills six hundred miles northeast of Calcutta. That same month, they surged across the Chindwin River into India. Most Indians realized that the Japanese were no liberators. Between the monsoons and the savage resistance of Indian troops, the Japanese invaders were battered. By summer they were out of India, leaving behind thirty thousand dead. The war that had looked so hopeless early in 1944 had completely reversed. The Japanese were being pummeled everywhere in the Pacific, just as Hitler's forces were being driven back in Europe. The defeat of both evils was imminent.

Gandhi was also finally out of prison.

"Britain is going to quit India," some told Amy.

The turnabouts defied belief. Was this yet another example of how good must spring from great suffering and pain? It seemed the war had drained Britain. In September 1944, newspapers carried reports that Gandhi and the leader of the Muslims were negotiating the nature of the independent state or states that would result from British withdrawal. The negotiations, as miraculous as they sounded, were not simple. Gandhi wanted a united India. But the Muslims wanted their own state, because they were afraid they would be overwhelmed by the more-numerous Hindus.

In May 1945, the terrible war ended. During the war years, Amy had raised her total number of books on India to thirty. The end of the war era signaled a great debt owed by Amy to Neela, one of her faithful nurses. In October 1945, she wrote Neela a loving letter:

> For nine happy years of nights you had care of your Amma, and I shall never forget. So often when there was pain, and you got very little sleep, your love helped me. You read to me and sang to me so sweetly, that sometimes sleep came while you were singing. I wonder how many times you sang, "The sands of time are sinking"? Well, darling, the sands of time have not yet run out. I have not yet reached the last clause of John 17:4. So ask for help for me still, strength and courage, and peace and joy, so that this room may be a Room of Peace to all. . . ."[1]

The clause to which Amy referred was "I have finished the work which thou gavest me to do." But her work was not yet finished. Nor was India's. Before 1945 ended, Britain announced it would give independence to India.

But was India ready? Month after month, Hindu leaders and Muslim leaders bickered. Speculation began. Some began to hoard food. Some began to starve. Riots broke out. Muslims killed Hindus. Hindus killed Muslims. Amy was amazed at the insanity of it all.

"And now the British say they will leave India in 1948 whether the Indians ever agree among themselves or not! Isn't that withdrawal inviting a bloodbath?"

Her own situation at times seemed insane, too. At one point in 1946, she realized she had not seen the sky in ten years! And yet the turmoil in India overshadowed all individual complaints. Hindus and Muslims squabbled and fought, but no one was prepared for what happened in Calcutta on August 16, 1946. Muslims had gathered for a rally in the great park called the "Maiden." Hindus agitated the Muslims. Scuffles broke out. Fighting spread like wildfire. Blood poured out of lives all over the streets of Calcutta. The killing was not by guns, but by the butchery of *lathis* and knives and hatchets. Deaths were silent, except for screams of pain. Thousands died.

"Can these wounds ever be healed?" wondered those at Dohnavur.

Indian leaders finally said no. In August 1947, two countries were born: India for the Hindus and Pakistan for the Muslims. Satan continued his work. Hindus began to coerce Muslims remaining in India to convert to their faith. Likewise, Muslims began to force Hindus left in Pakistan to convert to their faith. Again, killing erupted. Hindus overpowered the Muslims left in India and slaughtered them. Muslims slaughtered the Hindus left in Pakistan. Refugees by the millions fled to safety.

In February 1947, Amy was stunned to learn that

Murray's wife, Oda, insisted on an English education for the boys but refused to dump them in a boarding school. Amy remembered the pain of her own experience. Murray would either have to go to England or endure separation from his family. He decided to go to England. Amy did not take it well. Death would hardly have disappointed her more.

"No one is irreplaceable, some say," she wrote. "That is a shallow lie. Twenty years of knowledge of the East, all that is meant by fatherhood, cannot be passed on, as one might pass on a book or a garment. . .the sky is cloudy over India now. . . ."[2]

She still had enough strength at the age of eighty to get fired up. Upon reading that she wrote popular books she stormed, "Popular? Lord, is that what these books written out of the heat of battle are? Popular? O Lord, burn the paper to ashes if that is true."[3] Sometimes she was so tired that she fell into self-pity. "For years, patiently the prayer meeting went on praying for me," she recorded. "It does not seem to do so now. I was feeling the need of prayer very much, but to ask for it would be selfish. . . ."[4]

Many years before, in an Indian village, Amy had an experience eerily similar to one she had had in Japan. "We have heard much preaching from you about your Good News," said an open-minded elder. "But can you show us you live in Christ? And what is the power that comes with it?"

Well, look at the peace in our compound, she now reflected, *and look at what happens throughout India.* For India still smoldered, with murderous fights breaking out. Prime Minister Nehru lacked the moral power of Gandhi. In fact, Nehru, a British-educated Indian of the Brahmin caste, seemed at times more British than the British. Only Gandhi was able to stop the violence periodically through hunger strikes. Then in January 1948, Gandhi was murdered by one of his own Hindus. Gandhi was seventy-eight. How long would the bloodshed last?

At times now, Amy's strength failed her. On one morning in 1948, she wrote that she "woke feeling like ashes—as dull, as gray, in spirit—and all one ache in body."[5]

Would she have the strength to cooperate with Bishop Frank Houghton? Houghton was an old "China hand" from the China Inland Mission. He had been commissioned to write her biography. Amy felt just as George Macdonald had; the denial of self required that her personality be brought forth only so far as needed to advance good works. Anything more was intolerable. Still, if she had to trust someone to do her life, Frank Houghton was a good choice. She had corresponded with him many years. He and his wife had visited Dohnavur three times from 1943 to 1947. He had his hands full to be sure. He was awash in material. He arranged with Amy to send his product to her chapter by chapter for her critique. With God's help—and the assistance of Mary Mills and Neela—she would oblige him.

But on the evening of June 23, she slipped and fell in her room.

SEVENTEEN

A my broke her fall with her right arm.
Embarrassed, she told Neela, "Don't tell anyone—
I shall be all right in the morning."[1]

But Neela immediately sent for the doctors. "All right
in the morning" turned out to be a broken arm, a fractured
thighbone, and an injury of undetermined severity to her
hip. Amy hardly had the chance to feel sorry for herself.
Godfrey Webb-Peploe was in worse shape than she was.
His activity was now sharply curtailed because of failing
health. What had happened to Amy's successors? Her best
and brightest? Were they all going to fall before she did?
Ponnammal, Arulai, Murray. Now Godfrey?

December brought numbing news. Godfrey had a clot
in his right leg. He had to have complete rest. The clot
must not move. In the meantime, Amy could scarcely move
herself, as she confessed in a letter:

Year by year since 1935, when it seemed clear that recovery from the repercussions of the "accident" in 1931 was unlikely, I have asked that plans for the future, made clear to us in 1931, might be implemented. . . . Just now we are facing the unkindest thing, and the most dangerous spiritually, that the devil could contrive for us, and much prayer and thought must be spent upon it. . . .[2]

On February 19, 1949, Mary Mills came to Amy's side and said simply, "Godfrey is in heaven."[3]

No!

Amy seemed to weaken within seconds. What was going to happen to their wonderful enterprise for Christ? Where was the leadership? She was now eighty-one and very weak. On top of everything else, the new Indian government was making new rules and regulations all the time. The Fellowship now had to send out students to other schools just so they could get certification to teach and train the children at Dohnavur. To her closest confidants, Amy now spoke of the "crashing disappointments" of recent years. Only John Risk, an ex-naval officer, seemed to be developing into a leader.

But something wonderful happened.

Ponnammal's daughter, Purripu, began to emerge as a real leader. And so did Mimosa's son, Rajappan. Why had Amy doubted God? Did she think she personally had done all this? Praise God for His grace. All her old axioms came flooding back: "If the day ends in what seems failure, don't fret. Tell Him you're sorry. Even so, don't be discouraged. All discouragement is of the devil." "We don't need to press Him, as if we had to deal with an unwilling God." "We don't need to suggest to Him what to do, for He Himself knows what to do." It seemed that in her fatigue Amy had forgotten all her own advice. But it all would end for the good. God was the Master.

When one of her nurses came in to say good-bye before she left on furlough, Amy said, "We won't meet again in this world. When you hear I have gone, jump for joy!"[4]

By the time Amy turned eighty-three, she was truly immobile. She thought of little but her glorious Homecoming. Oh, praise God for the joy of the moment! Think who she would see: her mother, her father, the D.O.M., Thomas Walker, Ponnammal, Kohila, Mimosa, Arulai, Godfrey. The moment surpassed all her capacity to even imagine such joy. Once in a while she was brought back to the present. Had she heard someone speak of a headstone? She had told them emphatically that under no circumstances was she to have a headstone in God's Garden.

"And no coffin, just a wooden slab," she reminded her surprised nurse.

Amy heard whispers wishing she would tell them that she heard celestial music and saw Bunyan's marvelous Shining Ones and so forth. Hadn't she told the Fellowship, poor souls, that—except for flowers and songs of joy—she wished to go quietly? Had they forgotten that the Lord had told her in a dream, "I shall come to Thee in sleep—no rending good-byes—no distress to anyone"?

On January 18, 1951, He quietly kept His promise.

NOTES

CHAPTER ONE

1. Carmichael, Amy. *Rose from Brier.* Christian Literature Crusade. Fort Washington, Pennsylvania: 1933, p. 194. Copyright © 1933 by Dohnavur Fellowship. Used by permission.
2. Houghton, Frank. *Amy Carmichael.* Christian Literature Crusade. Fort Washington, Pennsylvania: 1953, p. 194. Copyright © 1953 by Dohnavur Fellowship. Used by permission.
3. Houghton, p. 2.
4. Elliot, Elisabeth. *A Chance to Die.* Fleming H. Revell. Grand Rapids, Michigan: 1987, p. 24. Copyright © 1987 by Fleming H. Revell. Used by permission.
5. Elliot, p. 22.

CHAPTER TWO

1. For further reading on this and other classic hymns, see Osbeck, Kenneth. *Amazing Grace: 366 Hymn Stories for Personal Devotions.* Kregel Publications. Grand Rapids, Michigan: 1990, p. 73. Copyright © 1990 by Kregel Publications.
2. Houghton, p. 115.

CHAPTER THREE

1. Osbeck, p. 284.
2. Elliot, p. 39.
3. Elliot, p. 41.

CHAPTER FOUR

1. Elliot, p. 44.
2. Elliot, p. 36.
3. Elliot, p. 36.
4. Houghton, p. 40.

CHAPTER FIVE
1. Houghton, p. 44.
2. Houghton, p. 46.
3. Houghton, pp. 47–48.
4. Elliot, p. 36.
5. Houghton, p. 53.
6. Houghton, p. 53.
7. Osbeck, p. 290.

CHAPTER SIX
1. Houghton, p. 67.
2. Houghton, p. 62.
3. Houghton, p. 59.
4. Elliot, p. 83.
5. Elliot, p. 82.
6. Elliot, p. 95.
7. Houghton, p. 72.
8. Elliot, p. 98.
9. Houghton, p. 74.
10. Elliot, p. 36.
11. Elliot, p. 104.
12. Elliot, p. 106.

CHAPTER SEVEN
1. Houghton, p. 83.
2. Houghton, p. 84.
3. Houghton, p. 84.
4. Houghton, pp. 84–85.
5. Houghton, p. 89.

CHAPTER EIGHT
1. Houghton, p. 97.
2. Elliot, pp. 146–147.

CHAPTER NINE
1. Houghton, p. 109.
2. Elliot, p. 142.

3. Houghton, p. 115.
4. Elliot, p. 170.
5. Houghton, p. 115.
6. Elliot, p. 178.
7. Houghton, p. 141.
8. Houghton, p. 134.
9. Houghton, p. 154.

CHAPTER TEN
1. Elliot, pp. 200–201.
2. Houghton, p. 177.
3. Houghton, p. 172.
4. Carmichael, Amy. *Gold Cord*. Christian Literature Crusade. Fort Washington, Pennsylvania: 1932, p. 178. Copyright ©1932 by Dohnavur Fellowship. Used by permission.
5. *Gold Cord*, p. 178.

CHAPTER ELEVEN
1. Houghton, p. 191.
2. Houghton, p. 191.
3. Houghton, p. 191.
4. Houghton, p. 239.
5. Houghton, p. 243.
6. Houghton, p. 203.
7. Houghton, p. 201.
8. Houghton, p. 195.
9. Houghton, p. 353.
10. Houghton, p. 196.

CHAPTER TWELVE
1. Houghton, p. 234.
2. Elliot, p. 268.
3. Houghton, p. 255.
4. Houghton, p. 255.
5. Carmichael, Amy. *Gold by Moonlight*. Christian Literature Crusade. Fort Washington, Pennsylvania: 1935, pp. 74–75. Copyright © 1935 by Dohnavur Fellowship. Used by permission.

6. Houghton, p. 265.
7. Houghton, p. 265.
8. Houghton, p. 323.
9. Houghton, p. 284.

CHAPTER THIRTEEN
1. Houghton, p. 290.
2. Houghton, p. 308.
3. Houghton, p. 335.
4. Houghton, p. 336.
5. Houghton, p. 348.
6. *Rose from Brier*, p. 10.
7. *Rose from Brier*, p. 88.
8. *Rose from Brier*, p. 53.
9. Houghton, p. 318.
10. Carmichael, Amy. *This One Thing*. Christian Literature Crusade. Fort Washington, Pennsylvania: 1950, pp. 79–83. Copyright © 1950 by Dohnavur Fellowship. Used by permission.
11. Carmichael, Amy. *Edges of His Ways*. Christian Literature Crusade. Fort Washington, Pennsylvania: 1955, pp. 194–197. Copyright © 1955 by Dohnavur Fellowship. Used by permission.
12. Houghton, p. 322.
13. Houghton, p. 322.

CHAPTER FOURTEEN
1. Houghton, p. 326.
2. Houghton, p. 332.
3. Houghton, p. 329.
4. *Gold Cord*, p. 80.
5. Houghton, p. 309.
6. Houghton, p. 307.
7. Houghton, p. 319.
8. Houghton, p. 318.
9. Houghton, p. 319.
10. Houghton, p. 318.
11. Carmichael, Amy. *Kohila*. Christian Literature Crusade. Fort Washington, Pennsylvania: 1939. Copyright © 1939 by

Dohnavur Fellowship. Used by permission.

12. *Kohila.*
13. *Kohila.*
14. Houghton, p. 311.
15. Houghton, p. 344.
16. Houghton, p. 355.
17. Houghton, p. 357.
18. Houghton, p. 358.

CHAPTER FIFTEEN
1. Houghton, p. 311.
2. Houghton, p. 311.
3. Houghton, p. 323.
4. Houghton, p. 340.
5. Houghton, p. 350.
6. *Gold Cord*, p. 133.
7. Houghton, p. 304.
8. Houghton, p. 352.
9. Houghton, p. 351.

CHAPTER SIXTEEN
1. Houghton, p. 353.
2. Houghton, p. 360.
3. Houghton, p. 329.
4. Houghton, p. 324.
5. Houghton, p. 312.

CHAPTER SEVENTEEN
1. Houghton, p. 373.
2. Houghton, p. 367.
3. Houghton, p. 363.
4. Elliot, p. 369.

FOR FURTHER READING

I. Two Exceptional Biographies:

Elliot, Elisabeth, *A Chance to Die: The Life and Legacy of Amy Carmichael*. Grand Rapids, Michigan: Fleming H. Revell Company, 1987.

Houghton, Frank L., *Amy Carmichael of Dohnavur*. Fort Washington, Pennsylvania: Christian Literature Crusade, reprint of 1953 original published in England.

II. Books by Amy Carmichael:

A. That chronicle Dohnavur Fellowship:
Things As They Are, 1903; *Gold Cord*, 1932; *Windows*, 1937; *Though the Mountains Shake*, 1943.

B. Of more specific interest:
From Sunrise Land, 1895; *Lotus Buds*, 1909; *Walker of Tinnevelly*, 1916; *Ponnammal*, 1918; *From the Forest*, 1920; *Ragland*, 1922; *Mimosa*, 1924; *Raj*, 1926; *Rose from Brier*, 1933; *Ploughed Under*, 1933; *Gold by Moonlight*, 1935; *Kohila*, 1939.

III. Excellent References on India:

Allen, Charles, *Raj: A Scrapbook of British India, 1877–1947*. New York: St. Martin's Press, 1978.

Mayo, Katherine, *Mother India*. New York: Harcourt, Brace & Company (in London: Allied Publishers), 1927.

Robinson, Francis, ed., *Cambridge Encyclopedia of India*. Cambridge University Press, 1989.

HEROES OF THE FAITH

This exciting biographical series explores the lives of famous Christian men and women throughout the ages. These books will inspire and encourage you to follow the example of these "Heroes of the Faith" who made Christ the center of their existence.

208 pages / Only $1.99 each!

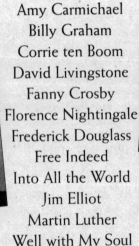

Amy Carmichael
Billy Graham
Corrie ten Boom
David Livingstone
Fanny Crosby
Florence Nightingale
Frederick Douglass
Free Indeed
Into All the World
Jim Elliot
Martin Luther
Well with My Soul